I Choose To Be Happy

A Practical Guide in Detoxing Your Emotions and Learning how to Love Life Again

Marie Houlden

Copyright

Copyright © 2020 Marie Houlden

Publisher: Marie Houlden (Self-Publishing)

Edition: First Edition July 2020

All rights reserved: No part of this book may be reproduced by any mechanical, photographic, or electronic process, or in the form of a phonographic recording; nor may it be stored in a retrieval system, transmitted, or otherwise be copied for public or private use—other than for "fair use" as brief quotations embodied in articles and reviews—without prior written permission of the publisher. The author of this book does not dispense medical advice or prescribe the use of any technique as a form of treatment for physical, emotional, or medical problems without the advice of a physician, either directly or indirectly. The intent of the author is only to offer information of a general nature to help you in your quest for emotional, physical, and spiritual well-being. In the event you use any of the information in this book for yourself, the author assumes no responsibility for your actions.

To protect the privacy of others, certain names and details have been changed.

Moral Rights: The author has asserted her moral right to be identified as the author of this book.

Cover Design: Martin Houlden (South Design Ltd)

Dedication

I dedicate this book to all those people who are seeking happiness in their life and are being brave enough to commit to the inner work.

Contents

Introduction and how to work through this book   12

Chapter one: The starting point

- Is this it for me?   16
- The wakeup call   22
- Is it time to create change?   26
- Do you even know what you want and who you really you are?   27

Chapter two: Mastering your emotions

- Stories that hold you back   40
- Limiting beliefs and stories from the past   44
- Are you really a positive person?   48
- Playing the victim   55
- How to embody a more positive approach to life   60

Chapter three: Self-acceptance and feeling like you're enough

- How to feel like you're enough and to accept who you are   64
- Your need to be perfect is exhausting you   74
- Stop allowing people to step over your boundaries   81
- Are you a recovering people pleaser?   88

Chapter four: Fear

- Fear creeps into all our lives   96
- Fear of making the wrong decision   105
- Fear of judgement, rejection and criticism   110

- Why other people choose to judge, criticise and reject others — 113
- Fear of failure — 118
- Fear of being happy and having everything you've ever wanted — 121
- Overcoming fear — 124

Chapter five: Self-sabotage and upper limiting

- Self-sabotage and upper limiting — 130
- What does self-sabotage and upper limiting look like? — 136
- Procrastinating — 137
- Blaming — 141
- Numbing out and avoiding our emotions — 142
- Fighting addictions — 144
- Attracting or creating drama, stress or conflict into your life — 145
- Playing down your abilities and gifts — 148
- Giving up — 149
- Blocking receiving — 151
- Why you sabotage and struggle to move past your upper limit — 152
- How to move past self-sabotage and overcome your upper limits — 157

Chapter six: Letting go and forgiveness

- Letting the past go, so you can create your future — 163
- Letting go of old beliefs — 168
- Letting go of the past — 171
- Letting go of what you thought life would, or should look like — 173
- Letting go of people — 175
- Forgiveness — 178

- Self-forgiveness   184
- How to let go of the past and practice
  forgiveness   189

Chapter seven: Allowing more into your life

- Allowing more into your life   196
- Are you willing to receive?   197
- Why you're unable to receive   202
- How to open up to receiving more   206
- The importance of self-care in choosing
  happiness   210
- Create your action plan, free resources and
  next steps   213

About the author   216

Acknowledgements   218

Introduction and how to work through this book

This book is for any woman who has ever wondered if this was all their life could ever be. It doesn't matter how old you are, what your relationship status is, whether you have children or not, or even what you do for a living. That dreaded feeling of *'is this it for me'*, is something that unites us all and this book is a resource in helping you to finally create a life that you love where it's easy to choose happiness.

When I created this book, it was never my intention to write something that you simply read to pass the time and then put down and forget about. This is a book that invites you to take an active role in creating your future and to think about what has brought you to this point. To do this, you need to be honest with yourself and complete the exercises that I share.

Often those quiet moments of reflection are when the most powerful insights and transformations happen. So please don't skip these questions and exercises. It may not always be pretty or easy and you may come up against resistance, but know that this is all part of the process of transformation and of creating a life that excites you.

We all live such busy lives, where we're always thinking about the next thing that has to be done. Give yourself the gift of time and know that you deserve to have this space to think about yourself and what you want and need. If you want your life to change, you need to change how you currently do things and put yourself first, because no one can do this work for you.

I would strongly recommend that you capture your thoughts in a journal or notebook, because as your self awareness grows and I can assure you it will, you'll start to see your own patterns emerging. This information is key in being able to fully understand yourself and to move forward more consciously.

The words in this book are more than entertainment; they help you to know that you're not alone with how you feel and the struggles you face, they will help you to create a life of pure happiness, where you're so clear on who you are and what you want. Each day you'll wake up excited about life again, because you're deeply connected to yourself and you feel alive, for some of you for the first time.

I'm sure some of you are thinking that there's no way you can do this and maybe it's not possible for you, but if I can, so can you. All it takes is commitment and belief in yourself. Know that I'm here with you, both through these words and through my belief in you too. I know we've crossed paths for a reason and if you'll let me support you, I know that you'll be able to choose happiness.

Like you, I've looked at my life and felt unhappy and dissatisfied and I'll openly share more of my own story in the first chapter. Over the last ten years, I've delivered thousands of private sessions and workshops to help people in their own quest for happiness. All of this has helped me to recognise what holds people back and also what works in creating change.
I also spent many years designing and delivering training for a large financial organisation, which is why I've chosen an interactive format for my book. I know that change has to come from within and words alone are not enough to encourage someone to change their behaviour, or do the inner work. They need to reconnect with themselves in such a way that staying stuck and unhappy is simply no longer an option.

Throughout this book I will be taking you through some key areas that are essential to explore and master if you want to create a life you love and be able to choose happiness with ease. My intention is that you would read the book in order, as each chapter builds on the last. Once you've read the book through once and you have all the information you need, you can then dip into chapters as you need them.

In each chapter, I'll share content for you to read and examples to bring things to life. It will help you to see that you're not alone in how you feel. There will also be questions for you to consider and reflect on. This is where so much transformation can take place, because finally you're in touch with yourself again. At the end of the book I'll be inviting you to create a simple action plan, where you capture anything that you're committing to over the next three to twelve months. As you answer the questions at the end of each section or chapter, just keep a note in your journal about the things you feel ready to heal and work on. It's also a good idea to be clear on any support you might need to make this happen.

You may find that I repeat some of my examples and questions, or pose them in a slightly different way throughout the book, I can assure you, this is intentional. Often we can't see what is right in front of us, and we can be quick to deny certain traits and behaviours in ourselves. Throughout the book I believe you'll see what you need to and those repeated examples and questions, will help with this.

By the end of the book you'll have a much better understanding of yourself, what you want from life and what needs to change; plus, you'll have an action plan to keep you focused and that helps you review your progress.

If you like the sound of this, then have your journal and pen ready, because it's time to begin.

Chapter 1

Is this it for me?

There comes a moment for so many women when they take a look at the life they're living and utter the words, *'is this really it'*?

Their life doesn't match the dreams and expectations that they held as a young and optimistic girl and they wonder how on earth they got here. They used to be so happy and yet now it feels like they're constantly chasing happiness and it always seems to outrun them.

For some it feels like right now life has beaten them. They've lost who they are, they can't remember the last time they belly laughed until they cried, and they have absolutely no idea where they're headed. Where there was once joy, passion and enthusiasm for life, there is now only exhaustion, overwhelm and the dread of all the demands that they know will be placed on them.

There's this nagging feeling within them that they were meant for more, that they should be doing more; but it's like having an annoying itch you can't quite reach. Part of them has given up on ever having what they want; the job, the career, true love, adventure, excitement, or a toned and healthy body. It feels too far out of reach and they just don't know if they have the strength to make it happen anymore. They are physically and emotionally exhausted, and at times disconnected to how they truly feel.

This empty feeling is simply a survival mechanism. They're blocking their emotions, because to be really honest with themselves is quite frankly, scary as hell. They're terrified by what might come up and, in those moments, choosing emptiness is the safer and easier option.

We've all done this, pretended that we're okay, we're coping and we're happy. The reality is, we're just not sure we can cope with the intensity of our emotions; we're scared by what could emerge and the impact this could have. Something, or someone from our past has made us believe that expressing and feeling strong emotions was not okay and acceptable, probably as it made them uncomfortable. So now it doesn't feel safe for us, or even allowed.

It doesn't matter what your current situation is; married, single, divorced, a house full of kids, an empty nest, or someone who never had children, these feeling can sneak up on us all, because life happens and things change, we change. The unexpected can be thrown at us and in those moments, we have a choice as to whether we sink or swim. Just so you know, sometimes it can take a whole lot of sinking, flapping our arms about like a crazy person and choking on water, before we finally decide that enough is enough.

I wrote this book so that other people would know that changing the course of your life, changing how you feel and being happy again is completely possible. I know because I did this while dealing with a massive amount of change. There were challenges in my life, which at times tested my sanity to the very core. I was displaced three times at work due to cost cutting exercises and quite frankly poor management, I had two miscarriages at twelve weeks, I moved six times in eight years, I separated from my husband, got back together with him, then left him again two years later and now I'm a single mum of two amazing kids and a growing business that brings me so much joy. I'm happier, healthier and more successful than ever. This book is more than just inspiration for what's possible, I want to show you how you too can choose happiness.

Throughout this book I'll frequently be telling you that I understand how you're feeling, and I really do. They aren't just words to try and make you feel better. Our situations and past may be different, but I've experienced the challenges of life, I've had low moods, I've dealt with frustration, overwhelm and the fear that nothing will ever change. I've played the victim, been irrational and refused to see what was right in front of me. But, despite all that was going on and how I was feeling, I had a dream and a vision for what I wanted my life to be. I knew nothing would get in the way of me making this a reality. Sure there were tough days, but I never stopped believing and trying, because in my heart there was a strong desire for more.

I craved a life of meaning and to do work that made a real difference to people. I wanted to be valued and paid well and I wasn't ever going to have anyone manipulate me again with empty promises. I wanted to be in love with my work, waking each day with excitement of what lay ahead. I didn't want to be one of those people who works every day, simply to get paid and to count the years until they could retire and really start living. I've never understood that mentality, because you're wasting the best years of your life, bound to something you have to give your time to every day and may not even enjoy.

None of us knows what the future holds and I have seen too many people get to retirement, only to experience ill health and be unable to do all the things they dreamed of. This is such a waste of life and I decided this was not going to be me. I was committed to choosing happiness and I wanted to enjoy life now.

Having a business that worked for me and fitted around my family was essential. I had young children and I was the primary carer, so it was important to me that I could be there for them. I didn't want to worry about working away or having to return to work full time if I wanted a promotion. I didn't want the drama of juggling sick days and don't even get me started on school holidays. I wanted to create a business that allowed me to put my children first and that would take away all this added pressure and stress. I had such a lot of motivation around my vision for this, because my children were and always will be, my priority.

I also wanted to release all that negative talk inside my head, telling me what I could and could not do. Boy she was mean sometimes and I was fed up with believing her. Like most people I really was my own worst critic, who needs enemies when you can just tell yourself how you're constantly failing, lacking and clearly aren't enough. I had spent years feeling like I wasn't enough because of other people's expectations of me and putting their needs first. I was tired, I was lost, and I was ready to come home to myself. I was done with over giving, over working and trying to be accepted by people who quite frankly didn't have my best interests at heart.

I dreamt of vibrant health and an abundance of energy, with a body that would never let me down. Working in a corporate environment with a massive amount of stress, pressure and manipulation made me so ill. The promise of pay rises and promotions if I just took on another project or more responsibility, along with being displaced three times meant my health was suffering. I had severe IBS (Irritable Bowel Syndrome) and I was on the verge of burnout. I was also struggling to fall and stay pregnant. After the second miscarriage, I knew something had to change. No job or company was worth my health, especially when they didn't even value me enough to be honest about their blatant discrimination, or respect my choice to have a family and work part time.

I wanted to experience a deep and meaningful love. My marriage was failing and I had become a shell of my former self. The spark in my eyes was well and truly gone, I didn't recognise the women staring back at me in the mirror. I had closed off my heart, because dealing with how I really felt was just too painful. Like many other women, I felt so lonely in my marriage, he was there physically, but emotionally he was far from present. We had lost that loving connection, we struggled to create moments of genuine communication and the mutual respect and support was seriously lacking. It was just two people living together because of the children. It was soul destroying and I couldn't accept that this was all I deserved.

Most of all, I wanted to believe in magic again and the infinite possibilities of this world. As a young girl I would spend hours reading Enid Blyton books and the stories that captivated me the most, were the ones filled with magic and far off lands. I would get totally lost in the words, in the characters and in the amazing things they were able to do. Somewhere along the way I stopped believing that anything was possible and that I could do anything, I wanted that feeling back.

My emotions had been getting the better of me for too long and I was tired of being triggered by people and things outside of my control. I was ready to accept what I couldn't change or control and to find myself again. Does this sound familiar to you? If so, you're most definitely in the right place.

We all have our own stories and experiences that have brought us to the current moment. This was my journey and my starting point and I'm sure that for every similarity, there will be just as many differences for you. In truth, the journey itself doesn't matter, it's how you choose to approach it that makes the biggest difference and that's what has brought us together. I believe there is a better way and I want to help you in your journey of choosing happiness.

From one overworked, overwhelmed and time poor lady to another, just know, you can change your life and you can be happy again and if you stick with me, I'm going to show you how. Over the last ten years, I have worked with hundreds of people, in thousands of sessions and as you can imagine, themes and patterns emerge. I want to share my insights and experience with you through this book. I know that change is possible, because I have walked this path and emerged the other side with a life, I am incredibly grateful for. I have also supported hundreds of other women in walking their own unique and individual path too.

Rest assured, there is nothing in this book that I have not tried for myself. I believe in practising what I preach. Do I mess up from time to time? Do I face fear, overwhelm and believe my own negative stories? Of course, but I always move past it and learn something new to bring to my own life and to my clients. Whether it's a greater depth of empathy, or a new technique to share. We're all on this journey of happiness together and I will be with you every step of the way.

More than ever before, this is the time for women to come together, to support one another, to accept each other and to cheer each other on. When I see how bitchy and competitive women can get, it actually makes me feel a little sad, because those people are missing out on something really special, the chance for genuine connection, friendship, support and understanding.

Before we get into the content of the book, there are a few things you need to do first. You need to commit to yourself and your dream of more. You need to want it so much that you're willing to face your inner demons, you're willing to take action and do the things that scare you and most importantly; you're committed to never giving up on yourself. I know this feels uncomfortable, especially when you've always put others first, or chosen the safe and easy path.

Know this, you matter and what you want and need matters. It's time to connect with your inner truth, it's time to find your voice and share who you really are. No doubt there will be plenty of old stories and beliefs that try and convince you that you aren't worth listening too and have nothing interesting to say, but you have to decide not to listen. Decide that you deserve to have a joyful and abundant life and that you deserve to be happy.

It's time to stop using excuses about when the kids grow up, when your parents don't need you, when you lose weight, or when your partner is more established and happier in their work. There will never be the perfect time and you'll always find excuses if you're not committed. Now is your time and when you truly believe this, passion, energy, abundance and opportunities will flow to you in ways you can't even imagine. The blocks will lift, your motivation and enthusiasm will return, and the world will become exciting again.

Finally, you need to give yourself permission to take action and this is probably the most critical piece of advice I can give. You simply won't achieve your goals if you don't take action. Not taking action, is like wanting to win the lottery without buying a ticket. Life wants to support you, but you have to meet it halfway. So, decide that your dream life is possible and that you will do everything in your power to make it happen. When you feel like this, it's easy to put one foot in front of the other and to just take action. You even begin to enjoy the journey.

So, are you ready to commit to yourself and choose happiness? Are you willing to commit to yourself, your dreams and your life? It doesn't matter what starts the fire in your belly, only that it's there and that you're ready to fan the flames.

The wakeup call

Let's start from the moment when we know that something, or everything in our life needs to change. That day when something just shifts within us, because the pain of waking up to the same life, day after day is simply too much. We look around and nothing makes sense anymore, we question how we got to this point and why everything looks the way it does.

For some people they just wake up and know that today is the day and suddenly they are spurred into action. For others, like me, it creeps up on them. It begins like a nagging ache or pain which is confusing because you can't pinpoint where it came from and then pow. For me it was like being hit with every emotion I have ever suppressed, I felt like I was in the middle of total chaos and couldn't quite breathe deeply enough. I wanted to cry, scream and shout all at the same time. Every moment of being unheard, unappreciated and feeling unloved came up for healing at the same time. It was not pretty, but it was time for me to face the truth.

Like so many strong women, I just got on with life and did what needed to be done, but I had lost my inner fire and fight. I felt that no matter what I did I would never be heard, respected or appreciated. I decided instead to get practical and focus on getting through each day. Life gave me the perfect distractions; the kids need sorting, the house needs cleaning, shopping must be done, I need to grow my business, before I knew it another week had passed. The emotional drain of living a life that was not in alignment with who I was, or what I wanted, left me too exhausted to consider that life could be different.

I knew that I was just surviving, and I also knew beyond any doubt that life had lost its passion and excitement for me. There were so many stories and beliefs from the past that were keeping me stuck and I could feel with every part of my body that it was time for some big changes. I didn't want to be defined by the past and those stories in my mind, I wanted more, I wanted to be happy and finally I had reached a point where nothing was going to stop me from making that happen.

When life has become a daily battle and you're simply trying to survive the day, then something has to change. Living this way is not sustainable and it's not fun. The physical toll on our body is so much greater than we realise, just think about all those people who have digestive health challenges, auto-immune disorders, hormone imbalances and depression. My experience with clients and my own body, has shown me that there is a strong connection between how we feel and what is happening in our body. Just something for you to consider when reflecting on your own health.

So, where do we begin with change and choosing to be happy? Well, the key is in working out which parts of your life are no longer working for you. Let me tell you about Sarah and what she shared with me:

Sarah heard the fireworks going off on New Year's Eve and began to cry. This was meant to be a time of celebration, of new beginnings and all she could do was feel overwhelmed with grief that another year had passed and yet life hadn't really changed from this time last year. There was a time when she had such hopes and dreams for her life, but now she felt like the biggest failure out there.

Love, life and success was meant to be easy wasn't it? But Sarah was lying next to a man that she no longer loved, with a business that was struggling. She was juggling all the responsibilities of her work, running a home, raising two young children and feeling like she was failing in every area of her life.

There was a lack of excitement and fun in her life and she felt like she had forgotten how to laugh, she wasn't even sure if she knew what funny was anymore. She was exhausted and overwhelmed by all the responsibility she was dealing with and the only way to cope with life was to shut her emotions down.

Her children were still young, and the rules of parenting seemed to change every day, what worked for one, definitely did not work for the others. Being a mum was what she had always wanted, but in the process, she had lost who she was. Now she felt defined by the label of mum.

The spark with her husband was long gone. They were two people living together and sharing the bills. Sarah was raising the children pretty much alone as her husband was very hands off. He felt it was her responsibility to do everything and made himself busy with work every hour of the day. In truth he was spending more and more time on social media, in chat rooms and basically connecting with anyone who wasn't his wife. The relationship with her husband had knocked her confidence so much that she wondered why anyone would value her and would want to listen to her. She felt broken.

That night was the start of the rest of her life. She finally began to listen to herself and her inner truth. Sarah spent time reflecting on what she wanted and needed from life, her business and her marriage and decided that she was going to try one last time to get her husband to hear her. When her husband proceeded to tell her that she was being unreasonable, or that he knew her better than she knew herself, she decided that he either had to step up and be a better husband and father or leave.

Unfortunately, it was the end of their marriage, but it has been the start of an incredible adventure of self-discovery and success for Sarah. Of course it was traumatic in the moment, but often the best things come from chaos and change. It all depends on how you view things.

You just have to ask yourself what would be more emotionally painful, being in a relationship where you felt unloved and at times invisible, or dealing with a few rough months of change. Sarah decided that a few tough months were easier than feeling dead inside for the rest of her life, because her husband couldn't see what an amazing woman he was lucky enough to share his life with. It was and will continue to be, his loss.

Women like Sarah really inspire me, because having been through a similar situation myself, I know it's not easy. There are lots of questions that swirl around in your mind and two of the most common I hear, are, *'Is it really the right time to create change'*, and *'Am I ready?'*

Two huge questions, ones, which I know I have personally asked myself many times. I often wondered if it was really the right time to make changes, or if I was simply a little bored with life. While my daily routine gave me structure and certainly helped with raising young children, I would question if I was fed up with knowing how each day would turn out, or if big changes were needed to really shake things up and get me excited about life again.

Is it time to create change?

For many people there comes a tipping point, when the pain of staying stuck is more painful than the fear of taking action, taking responsibility for your life and facing an uncertain future. Just think about the example of Sarah.

It's the moment when you realise that no matter how uncertain the future is, you would rather risk facing that, than stay living a life that was slowly killing your soul. You're simply not ready to give up on being happy and having the life you crave. I'm sure you're wondering how to apply this to you and if change is needed in your life.

Exercise

Take some time to reflect on the following questions and capture the insights in your journal. There are no right or wrong answers here, it's all about connecting with your truth and understanding how you feel right now. For some of you, it may feel hard or impossible to answer the questions, or to know how you feel. This is normal, so trust that more answers will come as you go through the book.

- Has life lost all meaning beyond the day-to-day grind?

- Are you stuck in what can only be described as a ground hog day? Are you going crazy with knowing how each day is going to turn out?

- Can you feel an ache inside that you are meant for more?

- Are you playing small, playing safe and not fulfilling your purpose or potential?

- Are you in alignment with your core values? When your life does not match these, it can feel very uncomfortable. For example, if you value genuine connections with people, yet you are spending time with people where all you do is have polite chit chat, you're soon going to get very frustrated and feel disconnected.

- Are you reading amazing books, watching things on You Tube, attending seminars and/or webinars, on how to create change and transformation in your life, but not putting it into daily practice? It had become entertainment, instead of a transformational tool.

- Are you being the role model you aspire to be for those around you, for example your children or perhaps friends and family members?

- Are you blaming other people and circumstances for how you're feeling and what you're achieving, or not as the case may be?

- Are you battling with a low level of anxiety, panic and a sense that you're off track?

- Do you fear that you're running out of time?

- Do you often think or say, *'I just want to be happy'*.

Do you even know what you want and who you really are?

The wakeup call is such an important part of our healing journey, but sometimes it can be hard to move past this stage, because although we know in our heart that change is needed and things can't stay the same, we have no idea what we really want from life. We crave happiness, because it seems that happiness itself is the answer, but in truth to be happy, we have to know ourselves.

I believe that knowing who you are and being fully connected to that, is one of the most important discoveries you'll ever make. It defines every decision and action you take and ultimately what your life looks like. When you struggle to really know yourself, it can affect every part of your life. You don't know what you like, what you stand for, or what you want to do in life. You begin to question everything and everyone, in the hope that you will get some answers or clarity.

I often ask clients to tell me about themselves, I ask them what they love to do, what they're passionate about, what they're good at and often they can look like a rabbit in headlights. The terrified look in their eyes, or the hesitation in their voice, tells me they don't know who they are. They try and pull some words together, anything to fill the empty silent space, but the truth is they have no idea how to connect to that part of themselves anymore.

Until now, life had beaten them. They had chosen to conform, forgetting who they really were in order to survive and fit in. Survive sounds like such a serious word, but one of the most basic human needs is to have connection, to truly belong and fit in. Thousands of years ago, having community was a matter of life and death, people could literally not survive alone. To try and guarantee connection and community, people will often stop doing or saying things that could cause them to be rejected or alone. The problem with doing this, is that over time it becomes harder and harder to connect to your own inner truth, and your own personal vision for life.

For such a long time, these women turned themselves into someone they no longer recognised, because it made others around them more comfortable. Perhaps they were in friendships or relationships where it was easier to compromise and people please, rather than to stand up for what they really wanted or believed in. When you suffer from low self-esteem, it can make you do the most crazy and stupid things for a peaceful and easy life, believe me I know.

When you're finally faced with the realisation of all the choices you made to simply fit in, belong and be accepted, lots of emotions can emerge; frustration, anger, disappointment and heaps of self-judgement. If this sounds like you, just allow yourself to fully feel into all of these emotions. As hard as it is, please don't judge yourself and don't make yourself wrong for what you said and did. You can't change the past and you made the best decision you could at the time. As painful as these moments of emotional chaos are, they are also life defining, because they made you ready for change and brave enough to demand more.

It's time to forget the past, the choices you made and everything you think you are. There is no rule which says you can't redefine yourself every day if you wanted to. I love the freedom that comes with this idea, every day I get to choose what that next version of me looks and feels like. This is what I tell my clients too, every day is an opportunity for a fresh start and a new beginning, so who do you want to be? You're so much more than you think and it's time for you to remember that.

When you're choosing to live from this place of alignment, you can't help but be happy. You're making authentic choices; you're spending time with people who bring you such joy and you're doing such fun things. Let's take a look at Anne's situation and see how easy it was to turn things around.

Anne was becoming increasingly short tempered with her husband and her children. She was feeling resentful at doing everything for them and not having any time and space in her life to refill her own cup. By asking a few simple questions, we were able to quickly establish that she was frustrated because no matter how organised she tried to be, she could never seem to fit in the gym and she needed exercise to get the endorphins running and to subsequently feel happy.

Her husband expected her to do everything around the house, sort the kids and work full time too, something had to give. She was feeling overwhelmed, underappreciated and was ready to snap. After having an open and honest conversation with her husband, they were able to agree on three times a week when he would take over responsibility for the children and she could get the workout she desperately needed. The end result is a happier woman and a happier marriage.

Sometimes the cause of our unhappiness or frustration is only a small thing, but when compounded, or when it's hugely important to us, it becomes a big deal. Never underestimate the importance of the small things you desire.

Self-awareness is essential if you want to be happy, because you have to be honest about what is, and is not working for you. No one else can give you that clarity. Creating a life you love needs your self-awareness and your self-commitment. Through reading this book and doing the exercises, I guarantee your self-awareness will grow.

I want to share a word of caution here, because this is often the point where many people give up and decide that all of this is going to require too much energy and effort. They identify where their life is not making them happy and then they panic. It seems too hard to make changes, to really get to know themselves and what they want. It's confusing and overwhelming to deal with their emotions and so they take the easy option and throw in the towel.

Being really clear on why your life can no longer stay the same is vital. Throughout this book there will no doubt be times when you want to run away and hide and not face how you really feel. You may get angry with what I am saying and think it's all nonsense, but if you have a strong enough reason why, and a clear vision, you'll be so committed to this process and to yourself, that nothing will stop you. You brought this book for a reason, so trust that you've got what it takes to create a life you love and that the goal of happiness is possible for you.

Exercise

To ensure you have all the motivation you need to see this through, I want to share a short visualisation exercise with you. Take a few deep breaths and wait until you feel calm and present, then:

- Visualise yourself one year from now, where nothing has changed in your life. Everything is the same. How do you feel, physically and emotionally?

- Now allow yourself to visualise three, five and ten years into the future where nothing has changed. Are your emotional reactions the same? What are you feeling? Who else does this impact?

- Now think about how you would feel if nothing were to ever change in your life, or with your emotional state. Are you okay with that? Could you still be happy and love life?

This exercise was a total eye opener for me, I didn't realise how much energy I was expending simply coping and surviving with life. The thought of spending even another year feeling this empty and shut down was too much for me. I was a shadow of my former self and quite honestly, I was wasting my life. Allow yourself to wallow in this exercise, because it's in these visions and how it made you feel that you'll find your motivation for taking action when things get hard.

I'm assuming that if you're still here and reading, that you're committed to choosing happiness and that a few words from me and some visions of the future, aren't going to scare you off. So, let's figure out what a happy and fulfilled life looks like for you. Remember, the process for getting clarity is different for everyone. It may come very quickly, or it might evolve as you learn more about yourself through reading this book. Just stick with it and stay committed, the answers will come, you just need to choose excitement instead of fear, because right now anything is possible for you.

Exercise

I want to share another exercise that I do regularly for myself. It helps me to check in with my inner truth and where I feel out of alignment within my life. When I am not aligned, I feel exhausted, frustrated, agitated and far from happy. I also know something is not right for me, when anxiety is coming up for no real reason. This is when I do a run through of every part of my life to see which area needs my attention and what change or action is required. Remember, when you're clear about what you don't want, you gain two important things; clarity over what you really want from life, because it's usually the opposite, plus the motivation to create change.

Try this meditation to gain more clarity within your own life and where you're out of alignment:

1) Close your eyes and take some nice deep cleansing breaths. In through the nose and out through the mouth. Just feel your body relaxing.
2) Let go of the thoughts of the day and give yourself permission to be fully present and set the intention of being open to clarity.
3) Know that you're deeply grounded, imagine roots coming from the soles of your feet and connecting you to the earth if it helps. This is especially useful if you have a busy mind.

4) Know that you're safe, imagine a bubble of energy all around you keeping you safe and supporting you as you go through this process.
5) Focus on those feelings of agitation, frustration, irritation, sadness or anxiety.
6) Ask your intuition to show you what area of life this is connected to. If you don't get a clear answer, then mentally picture each prominent area of your life. For example, health, work, money, relationships, hobbies and self-care, and see where the emotions intensify.
7) Ask yourself what can I no longer tolerate in my life? What are the things in life that are currently causing me the most emotional pain? What things, situations or people make me feel exhausted or drained?
8) Notice what you see in your mind's eye. Most likely there is a gap between what life currently looks like and what you truly want or desire. Also notice what memories or people appear in your thoughts. Pay attention to any other feelings and emotions that arise, as these can also hold clues. It could be that these are all things that require some inner work and healing so that you can move on with more freedom in your life.

Ensure you capture any insights in your journal, because it's always fascinating to see how things change over time and also to appreciate how far we've come too. It's easy to forget how all the little baby steps add up.

Exercise

Now that you have more clarity about where you're out of alignment and what isn't going so well, we're going to start exploring who you are, and what you want from life. The answers from these questions will help you reconnect with yourself and also make you think more about the work you choose to do and your purpose. If you're unsure of some of these answers, then it can be really interesting and helpful to seek the thoughts of those closest to you. Often other people can see what we can't, and they help us to appreciate the skills and gifts we overlook or don't see true value in.

Ensure you give yourself adequate time to answer these questions and capture your insights in your journal. Let's start with getting to know yourself better:

1. What am I passionate about?
2. What are my interests and where do I feel really alive? Who am I with?
3. What are my strengths and natural abilities?
4. Where do I lose all sense of time?
5. What did I most like doing as a child? What changed and why do I no longer do this?
6. What does fun look like for me? When did I last have fun and what was I doing?
7. What are my values? For example, mine include things such as honesty, growth, freedom, connection, making a difference, security and love.

I would suggest that you keep re-visiting these questions, because regularly observing your choices and your emotions will allow you to understand more about who you are. So many people struggle to answer these questions when they're put on the spot, but when you're in the middle of an activity or a situation it can feel crystal clear to you.

All emotions tell you something, you just have to be prepared to listen. When you're coming from a place of feeling alive, excited, passionate, joyful and full of love and wonder, then you know you're close to the real you. Don't forget that when you're feeling down or not enjoying something, this is also an amazing indicator. Think about what you really want in that moment, usually the exact opposite, and you'll know what you really want and desire.

If you want to gain more clarity, then use things such as EFT (Emotional Freedom Technique) or tapping, meditation, talking aloud as if you're coaching yourself, or writing in your journal. Personally, these all help me to process my thoughts and get to the root of what is bothering me, or they help me to understand what I really want from life. I strongly suggest you find a process that works for you.

Now that you have more clarity around your life, any gaps that you want to plug and who you are, we're going to start creating more clarity over what your ideal life looks like. I want to emphasise that this is all about you. What's important here, is your own definitions of happiness. Too often we get caught up in what other people are doing, how they're feeling, what they've achieved and what's important to them. We can often feel like if we are to fit in and be accepted, we must strive for the same things.

If you're looking for external approval and validation, you'll will end up frustrated and energetically exhausted, because you're totally out of alignment with who you are. Just because the big fancy house is important to your friend, it doesn't mean it has to be for you. Perhaps you value physical health or doing a job that you're passionate about. Variety is what makes the world exciting and it would be a terribly dull place if we were all striving for the same thing. If you find yourself going through the exercises and feeling confused and overwhelmed, perhaps even unclear about what you want, just know this is totally fine and normal. Don't judge yourself or make yourself wrong, notice it and ask yourself, *'why don't I know what I want'*, and notice what insights come to you.

For example, if your family always placed a big value on financial security, then they may struggle if you decide to give up your job and start your own business. Which is why you've resisted this path until now and chosen confusion instead. This is going to emotionally trigger them in some big ways. They're going to be scared 'for you' and will struggle to understand your decision. This is why some people just feel as if it is easier to conform, because then they don't have to deal with conflict or feeling as if they have disappointed someone else. It may feel safer, but this kind of life is soul destroying and it will sap your energy on every level.

Let me ask you, can you imagine a world where you came first, where your needs were met and whatever decisions you made were supported? I know, I know, you have a partner, children, family and friends who need you, but just indulge yourself. Imagine speaking and owning your truth. How does that make you feel? Excited, empowered, energized, nervous, unsettled or unsafe? Take notice of these emotions and any memories that come up for you, because these will begin to tell you a lot about yourself and why it's so hard for you to feel happy, and why sometimes choosing confusion is easier.

If you struggle, or feel resistance to picturing your ideal life, then it could be that you have some issues around low self-esteem and self-acceptance. Just notice what comes up and know that you are not alone with this, we'll be diving deeper into self-esteem shortly.

Allow yourself a good twenty minutes of uninterrupted time for the following questions, because this is your chance to daydream and really think about what your ideal life would look like for you, and how you want to feel. It's amazing how many of my clients go through this sort of process and come out the other side realizing that they were not even living or chasing their own dream.

Remember these questions are about your ideal life, not the life you're currently living. I want you to really let your imagination run wild, fully connecting with the life of your dreams. Don't censor yourself, or question if it's possible. If you struggle with what your ideal life would look like and feel like, here are some tips before you dive into the questions:

- What do you usually find yourself daydreaming about? What do you wish you had, or were feeling?

- What makes you feel incredibly happy, or makes you laugh?

- Where are you most jealous of others? Perhaps you look at your friends who appear to have happy and content relationships and you feel jealous, because this is missing in your life.

- What are you always moaning/complaining about? Think about the opposite. For example, I hate my boring job, could actually mean that you crave a job that makes you feel alive and where you feel as if you're making a difference.

Exercise

Now that you have some pointers, grab your journal, because it's time to get clarity on your idea life:

- Describe your ideal day? Where are you? What are you doing?

- How do you generally feel in this new life? What sorts of things do you do? What is your emotional state most of the time?

- What is your self-care practice like in your ideal life? For example, do you go to the gym, what is your diet like, how much sleep do you get; do you have time for meditation?

- Who do you spend time with? Where do you go? What do you do? How do the people in your life make you feel?

What are your relationships like? How do these people treat you?

- What are you doing as a job/career? How does your business, career or job make you feel?

- What kind of lifestyle do you have?

- How much money do you have in your ideal life and how do you feel about it?

- Where do you live? How does your home make you feel?

- Are there any situations or circumstances that are no longer present in your life?

How does it feel now that you've spent some time thinking about your ideal life? I know that when I first did this exercise, it left me feeling excited by my future, but also slightly flat, because life was nowhere near where I wanted it to be. I panicked at how impossible the task seemed to get me anywhere close to my ideal life. Once I let everything sink in, I knew I had work to do.

I recognised that at times it would be tough and that there would be moments where taking action would feel terrifying, but my commitment to myself and my dream life was stronger than my fear and because of this my life is now more amazing than ever and gets better every day. I believe the same can be true for you too.

Chapter 2

Stories that hold you back

We've finally made the decision to change our lives because we know that enough time has been wasted through our indecision, inaction and our belief that we should be grateful for our life and just accept things as they are.

We've begun to have these moments of absolute clarity of what we want the future to look like. We can picture the perfect house, a loving family, crazy cats and dogs, work that we're passionate about and fulfilling friendships. We can even see and feel a happier version of ourselves. In that moment, life holds so many possibilities and we feel like the most confidence and courageous women on the planet. Nothing is going to stop us from having want we want.

We start telling ourselves and others, that things are going to change, that finally we're going to get ourselves together and create our ideal life. We're excited, we're positive and we're connecting with a part of ourselves that we had long forgotten. Just when we find our stride, and we're taking action in putting this new life into place, we suddenly get paralysed with fear.

All of the negative stories in our mind want to be heard at once, telling us that we can't do this. We start remembering all the times we messed up and got it wrong, we start panicking over the future and we slip back into negative thinking and feeling powerless all over again. That sneaky voice in our head is doing anything it can to stop us from taking action and actually making changes in our life.

So what happened? Where did these thoughts and stories come from? Well, let's go back a little and get clear on what is happening inside our minds, because we all have our own little stories that hold us back from living the life we want and deserve. Quaint little tales that have been with us for so long that we have now mistake them for truth.

Each of us looks at the world very differently and this is because we all bring our own perspective to things. It's based on personal experiences, for example, our childhood, our role models, our friends, our education, our work and any other circumstances or situations we may have individually experienced. We're all unique and it's essential that you remember that, what causes an emotional reaction in one person, is unlikely to trigger another. No two people have ever walked the same path in life, and this is what makes people so fascinating, and at the same time so confusing.

It is widely believed amongst experts that most of our conditioning is formed before the age of six. Children before this age, are observing and watching everything and they take in the world subconsciously. From this they give things meaning and it eventually turns into their truth. From this place of truth, they form opinions and make decisions. Let me share some examples for you.

Carla grew up with a father who would only give her attention when she excelled at something, the rest of the time he had very little time or patience for her. As she grew older, he would become increasingly critical. If she achieved an A, he wanted to know why it wasn't an A+. Carla grew up feeling like she wasn't enough and nothing she would ever do, would be enough.

This led to perfectionism, overachieving and burn out. Carla was filled with self-judgement, criticism and self-doubt and it impacted every area of her life. She constantly thought she was overweight, that she should have achieved, and she had a habit of people pleasing with everyone in her life, simply to avoid rejection, criticism and judgement. Despite having an amazing husband who adored her, she couldn't accept how amazing she already was.

We all like to be right, and unfortunately, we will block out the things that would prove us wrong. For Carla she couldn't see or accept that she was already enough and didn't need to work so hard, lose weight or constantly over give.

Then we have Brenda who grew up with a father who was always working and who rarely helped her mother with housework, or child rearing. She grew up with the belief that you have to work hard to get money and that women will always do the majority of the housework. Can you guess how this impacted her? She became a workaholic herself, sacrificing her work life balance and self-care and she attracted a partner into her life, who didn't support her when it came to household chores and raising the children. Which meant she ended up working even harder.

When you stop and really think about your own upbringing and the patterns we recreate, it's quite frightening and very limiting. We're living our version of normal, even if it's not healthy or good for us. Plus, for many of us there is this internal drive to recreate the past so that we can try and make it better this time around.

As a parent myself, the concept that a person was shaped before the age of six blew me away. To say that I felt a huge amount of responsibility is an understatement. I can remember at times, being obsessed by what I was saying or doing with the children, as I didn't want to adversely affect them. Eventually I came to accept that you can be the best parent in the world and still not give your child all the lessons they need. For example, the parent who never allows their child to fail by continually coming to their rescue or preventing them from even trying. As an adult life will be a real shock for them, because failure becomes excruciating, simply because they never had the opportunity to learn resilience or how to bounce back.

How and why you see the world as it is, is such an important starting point, because then we can begin to unpick why some people feel like they deserve things such as success, happiness, health and love and why others just don't. At times this may get very uncomfortable and all sorts of emotions may come up. As I always say to clients, *'just observe what comes up and how you feel, be curious and intrigued and never ever judge yourself'*. To follow this advice, just allow yourself to feel into your emotions, and then take note of them. Self-awareness is so powerful and it's the key to change and being more empowered.

It would be easy to feel regret about the past and feel mad at yourself for decisions and choices you made, but we're all on a journey. We learn and heal at the perfect time for us, and ultimately it's not a race or competition. This quote sums up how I feel about my own journey to healing and becoming more self-aware, and it may be useful for you too:

"Your journey has moulded you for your greater good, and it was exactly what it needed to be. Don't think you've lost time. There is no short-cutting to life. It took each and every situation you have encountered to bring you to the now. And now is the right time."
Asha Tyson.

Your past and everything you've experienced has brought you to this point in time and made you the woman you are today. Now that you can understand that a little more, we're going to explore three key areas, before I share some practical tips at the end of the chapter. The information I will go onto share will of course be useful and thought provoking, but often the biggest breakthroughs come when you work through the questions. The space you give yourself to just think about the questions and feel into the answers, is priceless. Insights may emerge which you may never have been aware of before, or had previously suppressed. Don't let this book be just another form of entertainment and distraction from a life that doesn't fulfil you. Let's explore these stories and limiting beliefs a little more.

Limiting beliefs and stories from the past

We already know that our younger years have a huge impact on us and by the age of six we've already absorbed many subconscious beliefs about ourselves, both in terms of our capability and who we are as a person. These beliefs can often limit us in terms of our accomplishments, because we have accepted them as a truth for what is achievable in our life and what is acceptable behaviour based on others expectations of us.

Regardless of where the limiting beliefs come from, they are heavy burdens and they can impact how positive we feel. We may try and act all confident but inside we're still that scared little girl, who is terrified of being seen, being rejected or being criticized.

These limiting beliefs can stop us from having the life we truly desire, because we question if more is possible for us. These stories can keep us stuck in relationships, friendships and jobs we don't enjoy, or aren't' good for us, because we can fear this is all we're worth. We make all our decisions from a place of fear, rather than from a place of truth about who we really are and what we really want.

When we're caught in a cycle of low self-belief, we can almost believe that nothing will ever change, and that life will always be this way. It is only an illusion and if you're prepared to do the inner work, you can break free and get things back on track.

One of the things that I see time and again is women struggling with a lack of self-belief. It truly breaks my hurt to watch them question themselves, their abilities and what they're capable of in life. I can see how amazing they are and yet they have this distorted view of themselves. I understand this, because I've been there too and even now I can have moments of total self-doubt.

Those moments can make you feel so alone, because you look around and all you see are people who have their lives together and are brimming with confidence. You're desperate to feel like that, but instead you're sitting with this sense of self-loathing and self-criticism. We talk to ourselves in a way we would never dream of with another. We're cruel, unkind and relentless. We judge every flaw; physically and emotionally until we're too exhausted to take action and make changes. We're exhausted from running a race we can never win and part of us has accepted that life will never change for us.

The journey of transformation is not always an easy one. You may find that you experience frequent resistance to exploring emotions and accepting what is. This is your mind trying to keep you stuck, because even though you're frustrated with life, there is a dark comfort in it. Everything is familiar and familiar feels safe.

There are so many different reasons that a lack of self-belief can rear its ugly head; from beliefs brought forward from childhood, to traumatic events that happen to us as adults. Some people are so deeply entrenched in negative emotions, that they've come to believe that this is the way life will always be.
 This is my promise to you, I will believe in you and your potential even when you struggle to see and feel the light in yourself.

When working with clients I am always very conscious of the language they use, because this tells me so much about their mindset. I'd like to share the following list with you, to see if you can begin to recognise words that slip into your own thoughts and conversations every day. A useful exercise is to monitor your thoughts and your conversations throughout the day, to see what keeps arising and what these limiting thoughts are connected to:

- I can't
- I shouldn't
- I'm no good at
- I'm not as good as
- I don't have enough time

- I'm too old/too young
- I'm not attractive enough
- I'm not enough
- I'll try

As you take a moment to consider how using these words and the associated beliefs, has limited your life, let me share some client stories.

Beth was an amazing life coach, but she was scared that she was too old to change career at fifty-five. Retirement wasn't too far away and the sensible part of her was telling her to just wait it out. Her heart ached to help others and she did it so naturally anyway, but her stories about being too old and not qualified enough held her back. This led to years of procrastination, until she finally decided enough was enough and she was doing this.

Or what about Lisa who wanted to share her gift as a healer, but was convinced she wasn't good enough and that no one would choose to work with her, pay her, or even listen to what she had to say. She was constantly comparing herself to others and couldn't see how amazing she already was.

When we use these limiting words, even if only in our own minds, we're questioning everything about who we are as a person. We've decided that we're not enough and so we question if we deserve the good things in life; a loving partner, money in our bank account, and a fit and healthy body. There is a constant inner critic in our mind making us doubt ourselves, which impacts our choices, the actions we take and our confidence.

By allowing these stories to play a dominant role in our thoughts and conversations, we're choosing to be a victim of what life throws at us. I know this is hard to hear, because I fought against this too. I didn't want to be labelled as a victim and someone who couldn't take ownership of who she had become and everything that had happened. The moment I finally realised that if I wanted my life to change, I needed to change my beliefs and thoughts, I became truly empowered and in control of my life again. It was only then that I could create the success and happiness I truly desired.

Exercise

It would be easy to feel overwhelmed right now, but just know this, you get to decide what you want to believe from this moment on. If you find your beliefs are limiting you and your potential, ditch them and choose a new belief. You really are that powerful and it really can happen that quickly. Let's start looking at you, by considering the following questions. Make sure you capture your thoughts and insights in your journal, because through the course of these chapters, you will see patterns emerging:

- Where are the limiting beliefs or stories in your life? What have you told yourself that you can't do, or shouldn't do? Think about all the words I shared above and some of the key times you have used them.

- What is the impact of believing these limiting beliefs? In particular, think about the things you're not doing. Do you have regret? If you find yourself becoming emotional during this, please don't judge yourself, allow yourself to feel whatever is present. These emotions are telling you that this is important, and you need to pay attention.

- Ask yourself if there is a deeper reason for keeping these limiting beliefs? For example, do you have a fear of failure, fear of rejection etc. We'll be looking at fear in a later chapter, but ultimately, beliefs can keep us safe and at times this feels more important than the changes we crave.

- Are these beliefs affecting more than just you? Think about the impact these beliefs might be having on your relationships and with your children. What would be the impact on you and your life if you could leave these beliefs in the past?

- Which of these limiting beliefs are you ready to start working on today?

When I first started exploring the following questions, I was astonished to see that the beliefs and stories I had carried for years were not even mine. They were handed down from my parents and other role models. I assumed they must be true, because they were in my head and that this is the way life was supposed to be.

As always, make sure you're capturing your answers and thoughts in your journal. All of this information is so valuable in creating your plan for the future and I'll be inviting you to pull this all together in the final chapter.

Are you really a positive person?

Now that we have some clarity around the stories holding you back, it's time to think about how you approach the world and life.

Very often people will tell me that they are a positive person and although I hear all the right words, something just doesn't feel right to me and this is when I know that there's a mismatch between what they're saying and how they really feel.

"Your unconscious thoughts and emotions, both from the present and the past, are always broadcasting out to the world". Dr Barbara De Angelis.

For sensitive people like myself, we can pick up on the unspoken and even if you are trying to fake it until you make it, we can feel that something isn't quite right. This is a gift I truly treasure, as it helps me to uncover things with my clients that could be missed if I relied on language alone.

Amanda would constantly talk about how positive she was as a person, especially considering all she had been through in life, yet she was always moaning, complaining and seeing the worst in people and situations. In the nicest possible way, she was a total drama queen, always going to the worst-case scenario. Over the years I think it had become an ingrained habit and I'm not even sure she realised she was doing it. I believe it was a way to feel important as people listened to her and it gave her the attention she craved. Long term this is not an ideal strategy, but short term it seemed to be working for her.

Let's look at another example around money. Emily seemed to be doing all the right things when it came to attracting money and releasing her money blocks. She was saying daily affirmations, she was visioning the future and expressing gratitude, but money was just not flowing to her. The problem was all the old unresolved emotions, such as anger, fear, negativity and doubt, and the energy of these emotions were leaving a very distinct mark on her life.

Telling yourself and others you're a positive person is not enough, because your actions will always speak louder than words. The way to achieve genuine lasting positivity, is to be honest with how you feel and to deal with your emotions. There is so much pressure to be positive all the time, especially with the noise of social media and while I'm all for being positive, I don't believe in masking emotions and denying how you feel. The way to true positivity is acceptance, processing, releasing and then taking the necessary action.

Affirmations are another controversial area for me, because I know that many people rave about them. Personally, I believe you can say affirmations till the cows come home, but if don't release and heal those dark and heavy emotions from the past, you're always going to feel as if you're swimming upstream. Plus, people will sense the lack of authenticity within you.

So what can you do about it? Well, you need to start doing the inner work and deal with those heavier and dark emotions. I know it sounds like a drag and for some of you outright terrifying, but if you want to have that amazing life, you have to begin within yourself, because you'll never be able to full control anything outside of yourself. It really is that simple.

Facing your feelings takes a great deal of strength and courage, and I have an immense amount of admiration and respect for anyone willing to do this.

Before we begin to look at you a little more, I want to stress again that we'll all go through challenging times in life and it's essential that you allow yourself to fully feel into the emotions that these situations and circumstances bring up for you. There are times when it's not appropriate or necessary to pretend that all is well. So please don't think you have to put on a mask to make it easier or more comfortable for others, or because you worry about bringing other people down.

Through my work with hundreds of clients and my own personal experience, I have seen time and time again that there is a strong connection between the mind and the health of the body. I know how detrimental suppressed emotions and feelings can be for your physical health. Many of my clients have had challenges with their digestive system, or with burn out, and part of this was because they suppressed how they really felt. They tried to carry on with life, never giving themselves the time or space to admit, or express their true feelings.

So what does it mean to be positive? Well, it's all connected with how you react to the events, circumstances and people in your life. Some people will always react and speak negatively, while others take a more positive approach. Have you noticed which ones tend to be happier and are nicer to be around?

No doubt there are people in your life who you find it hard to be around. For some reason they drain you of energy and you can't wait to get away from them. Often this is because they look at the world and what is happening in their life in a negative way. They feel like everything is happening to them, that life is not fair, that they have no choice, and that they're powerless. They see the world, as if their glass is half empty and they're constantly terrified by what else might happen. Does this remind you of anyone in your life?

Consider how it feels to be in their company and how you feel when you leave. For me the relief is incredible. Finally I can breathe again, my body feels expansive and life feels good. People like this constrict me so much and over the years, I have had to let go of friendships I once valued because they have become so toxic to me. I'm also very careful of who I choose to spend any time with. Lunch with a negative person or someone who wants to talk at me rather than with me, can impact my energy levels for the rest of the day and my time is too precious to allow that.

The exercises coming up are going to help you get clear on your own natural reaction to things. It's about taking some honest reflection time to see what habits you have formed; where you need to stop being negative and where you might need to face your true emotions.

I've seen incredible things happen when people work on the emotions that are affecting them, so as I've stressed before please don't judge yourself and please be honest. You're doing yourself no favours by being defensive and declaring that there's nothing wrong with you and it's everyone else who has the problem. If people keep avoiding you, giving excuses not to spend time with you and generally seem disinterested in what you have to say, then you really need to look within. Other people are not the problem here, you are.

The questions in the exercise will help you increase your levels of self-awareness as we know this is where power lies. If you can see for yourself what you're doing and then choose differently, you're suddenly in control of your life and no longer giving your power away to things outside of your control. It's also helpful to see where your negative thinking comes from. If you grew up in a very negative family, it's very likely that this way of thinking and looking at the world was considered normal. The past does not have to define your present moment, or your future.

Exercise

Before we get to the main exercises, I'm curious, right now, would you consider yourself a positive or negative person? It's okay if you're not sure, but maybe reflect on the reasons behind your answer.

As always ensure you set some time aside to give these questions the attention they deserve and make sure you capture your responses and insights in your journal.

Look at the statements below and observe your immediate thoughts and feelings. This is not about what you think you should say or think, this is about finding out whether your natural reaction is to be positive or negative. Some of these questions will be more relevant to you than others, but try and answer them all.

1. You had been planning on going away on a much needed holiday and your partner says 'I can't take the time off work anymore'. Do you fly off the handle, scream and cry and declare that they're a selfish person who doesn't truly care for you; or do you feel the disappointment but move onto finding a solution?
2. You win £50 on the lottery. Are you happy and grateful; or do you instantly wish it was more?
3. Your partner gives you an unexpected present or does something nice for you. Do you feel very loved and cared

for; or wonder what they've done wrong, or what they want?
4. You go out with friends and they start moaning about their partners. Do you join in; or do you try and change the subject to something more positive?
5. During your conversations with people, what do you generally talk about? Are the topics negative, or positive?
6. You're struggling with your diet and weight and you desperately want to lose half a stone. Do you decide there's no point in trying to lose weight as no diets work, exercise isn't for you and everyone is overweight in your family anyway, so why fight genes; or do you create a healthy eating and exercise plan and stick to it?

When you reflect on your responses, what emotions and thoughts came up? Were any of the emotions reoccurring? Are you surprised by your insights? For each of us we will of course have people, situations and circumstances that can pull us into negativity. The beauty of being honest about this and noticing how it affects us, is that we have been given an opportunity for growth and a very clear indication of where we need to begin our work.

Now that you've started to understand your natural reaction to things, please look at the following questions.

Exercise

Make sure you capture all your insights in your journal.

1. List all the qualities you can think of, for a positive person. Maybe have someone in mind who oozes positivity in your opinion. What is it that they say, do, or how they come across that makes them positive? How do you feel when you spend time with them?

2. Now, list all the qualities of a negative person. Again, have someone in mind. Really go to town on what they say and do that makes them negative and think about how this impacts you.

3. Look at these two lists carefully and see if you can spot your own traits on there. Are you starting to see potential areas of growth for yourself? What changes are you inspired to make?

4. The next step is to make a list of the people who have had a significant impact on your life, and those that you spend the most time with? Now, make a note as to whether they're a positive or negative person.

5. Are you surprised by what you see? Who do you need to spend less time with, or perhaps set more loving boundaries with? We'll be exploring your relationship with others and boundaries in the next chapter, so don't worry if you feel unsure about this topic at the moment.

Once you've answered the questions fully, you'll have some really insightful information about yourself and those who you spend time with. You might even have some things to implement, which will help you to feel happier. It could be that you feel inclined to focus on making changes straight away because being more observant of yourself and making those subtle mindset shifts, feels quick, easy and simple to implement. The ideal situation is that you stop your negative thinking before it takes hold of you and becomes embedded in your thinking and natural way of doing things. We also want to catch the negative thinking before it escalates into you playing the victim, which is what we're about to explore next.

Playing the victim

A very common trait of negative people is to fall into victim mode and play the victim. Now before we dive in, it's important to say, that I am referring here to a state of mind, and it's not within the scope of this book to address the serious issues of true victims and the trauma they have experienced. In this book, we're going to be looking at what it means to choose to be a victim of life, when other options are open to you and what those traits can look like.

I love this quote from Steve Maraboli, *'Today is a new day. Don't let your history interfere with your destiny! Let today be the day you stop being a victim of your circumstances and start taking action towards the life you want. You have the power and the time to shape your life. Break free from the poisonous victim mentality and embrace the truth of your greatness. You were not meant for a mundane or mediocre life!'*

Playing the victim, being a victim, or having a victim mentality, is ultimately about giving away your power and saying that you have no control, or choice over your current situation. It's about believing that everything in life is happening to you and you're the poor defenceless person who can't do a thing about it. It's often a role played, because it gives an excuse to avoid change and difficult situations and ultimately you can blame something outside of yourself for everything that is happening in your life. Doesn't sound very attractive does it?

Before we explore why people would choose to adopt the role of a victim, I'll share some traits and examples. I'm sure you'll be able to spot people in your life who do these things and if you're honest, you'll probably identify parts of yourself in there too. Remember, no self-judgement. We can't change the past, but we can rewrite our future. Feeling any kind of truth in these examples, either towards yourself, or towards someone in your life, is an opportunity for growth.

These are some examples and traits of those adopting a victim mentality:

- They will often moan about the same things over and over, but will do absolutely nothing to change things. As I'm sure you know, it's very tiring and frustrating to be on the receiving end of the same conversation and knowing exactly how it will end. It's like watching a bad movie, with a depressing ending, why subject yourself to it?

- Victims will often take no action, blaming everything and everyone under the sun for why it just isn't possible for them. All you'll hear are rejections to any solutions you offer, and excuses for why they couldn't or didn't take action. After a while you stop trying to help them and if you can, you avoid them.

- Blaming others for their situations and how they feel is very common. Just think about the person who blames their partner for everything. I hold my hands up and say that I used to do this, I would blame my husband for how unhappy I was, but ultimately, I always had the choice to leave.

- They'll see no way out of their current situation, or anyway that they could change how they currently feel. They're shut off to suggestions and to seeing things differently. They're choosing to feel powerless.

- They will generally be very negative about everything and everyone, just think about the client I mentioned earlier.

- Everything is unfair and unjust, even when it's not. They convince themselves that they've been treated unfairly, because they just can't accept responsibility for their actions and choices.

- Often there is indecision, which leads to no choice being made. However, in choosing not to decide, they are deciding.

- They'll often claim that other people are being selfish and don't care about them , simply because other people are now asserting their boundaries and are refusing to spend time with them, or to listen to the same list of complaints on repeat.

There will of course be moments when we've all played the victim, the key is in identifying this and snapping out of it quickly. When we believe we have no choice and that things outside of us influence our life, we're forgetting how much freedom we have and how powerful we are. I don't know about you, but I'd rather face all of the bad choices I made and take responsibility for them, knowing that I can choose to create a life of magic and meaning in the future.

So why do we choose to play the victim, especially if it means playing small with our life and potentially alienating those around us? It's a good question, and there are various reasons that people would shy away from feeling empowered with their life and taking action and claiming responsibility. Here are some common reasons that I see every day with clients and those around me:

- It's become a habit. This is what they've always done and so it feels completely natural for them. It can also be connected with how they see the world, for example their glass is half empty, or they're holding onto the belief that nothing ever works out for them. To suddenly decide you are in fact powerful and have the ability to change your life, is too terrifying for some to even contemplate.

- They're meeting some of their deeper psychological needs by being a victim, for example, they get attention from others. This sounds crazy, but some people are so desperate for attention, which is ultimately a need to feel important to others and to be loved, that they will put themselves in the position of being a victim. Remember my example of Amanda.

- It can make them feel safe, because they don't have to face the uncertainty of conflict if they choose to speak up, the fear failure if they take action, or worry over making the wrong decisions. It's much easier to stay powerless.

- They're waiting for something, or someone to come and save them. It could be that they don't believe they can do this for themselves, they could be scared to make changes, or perhaps they have become used to always being rescued or saved.

- It's also incredibly hard to look inwards and take responsibility for everything you've ever said or done. There could be an immense amount of guilt or shame to address and so it's much easier to attack outwards and deflect. The trouble is when you do this, nothing changes.

Let me share Judy's situation. She knew she'd played the victim in the past and part of this was being truly scared to ask for what she wanted and needed. She held onto a fear of her request being unheard, denied and she felt uncomfortable in asking for something that the other person might find hard to hear. I'm sure this is something that all people pleasers can relate to. Eventually she reached a point where she didn't want this to impact her marriage anymore and she would rather choose a few moments of discomfort, over this destructive habit. She found her voice and her power again and luckily her husband was committed to truly listening.

Once we begin to understand the deeper reasons for choosing to adopt a victim mentality, then it becomes easier for us to break free from this habit and to have compassion for others who are still on this path. I am not saying that it won't be hugely frustrating at times, but we're all on our own journey.

Exercise

We're now going to take some time for inner reflection around playing the victim. Don't be surprised if by working through the following questions, it brings up emotions such as shame, guilt and embarrassment, because no one likes to think of themselves as choosing to play the victim. This is all totally normal and part of the process.

The questions will be immensely enlightening, as they give you the chance to see which people, situations and circumstances in your life, can potentially encourage the victim in you. This information is priceless, because it's a game changer for the future. Once you identify your triggers, you can choose differently and begin the process of healing.

I'm also going to add in a question about other people who could be playing the victim in their own life and impacting you. If you're a highly sensitive person and you tend to people please, over give and you help others more than you should, then it's essential to know that it's not your responsibility to fix, save or rescue anyone else. Their happiness is their own responsibility.

Reflect on the following questions and as always capture any insights in your journal:

- Thinking about your own life, can you identify where you have played the role of a victim in the past? Reflect on who can trigger this response in you.

- What sorts of behaviours did you display? For example, poor me, blame, avoiding conversations, avoiding taking action or refusing to take personal responsibility.

- Can you identify any reasons that you might have chosen to adopt a victim mentality?

- Are there people in your life, who tend to adopt the victim role? Can you start to see what they're underlying motivation might be, to gain attention or sympathy, to get others to save them, or make them happy? Incidentally this is a form of emotional manipulation and control. As mentioned above, it's not for you to save or rescue them. Ask yourself if there is anyone that you need to set a more lovingly boundary with, or perhaps even move away from completely?

- What actions could you take to reclaim your power, set loving boundaries and let go of your own victim tendencies?

When you reclaim your power, take full responsibility and remember how powerful and amazing you already are, life will begin to get very exciting, very quickly.

How to embody a more positive approach to life

Now that we've finished exploring your mind, thoughts and habits, and you have all this information and awareness about yourself and the things that triggers your negative thinking; it's time to look at the future and how you can take all this forward. The following suggestions will help you to become not only more positive, but also allow you to feel and experience more joy and abundance in life. These are things you can commit to immediately, as well as things you can add to your journal and action plan:

- Take responsibility for your life and make things happen. No one can do this for you. Remember only focus on the things that you can change. There's no point wasting your energy in trying to change things that are out of your control, like the past, or even other people.

- If you have problems that need to be dealt with in your life, stop putting them off and hoping they'll go away, or wishing that someone will come and save you. Write everything down that is occupying head space and try and tackle one thing at a time, you'll feel so empowered because you're taking action.

- Don't take on the role of a victim and blame others for why your life doesn't look the way you want it to

- Accept that bad things sometimes happen, it's how you respond to those things that make a difference. Of course, you need to feel into the emotions of the bigger emotional pieces in life and it would be wrong to suggest otherwise, but it doesn't mean you have to stay stuck in pain for eternity.

- Stop the moaning, criticising and complaining. Not only does this drag you down and gives unnecessary energy and attention to the things you're not happy about, it also affects those around you. No one wants to spend time with someone who drains them. Again, I am not talking about the times when we need support, I am talking about being negative for the sake of conversation. Think about the quality of your conversations and if necessary, steer the conversation towards more positive things.

- Be grateful for what you have in life, it's impossible to be negative while also being thankful for the roof over your head, your family, your friends etc. We'll talk more about gratitude in our final chapter.

- Protect your personal boundaries and don't spend time with people who bring you down and cause you to negatively spiral. Sometimes you have to let go of unhealthy and toxic relationships and friendships. I know this is hard when it comes to family members, but maybe this is initially about reducing the time you spend with them. We'll come onto boundaries in the next chapter.

- Try not to judge others, as often this involves negative emotions and feelings. You've no idea what path they've walked in life and you're wasting energy by directing your judgements at them

- Be mindful of watching the news. It's full of hate, violence and negativity and it creates fear. Remember it only reports a small percentage of what is going on in the world. Also consider the TV shows you allow yourself to watch. Is it uplifting and inspiring, or dark and depressing?

- Enjoy life, smile, dance, sing, do activities that fill your heart with joy, engage in conversations with people and just connect. Fun is good for the soul.

These are just a few simple examples to give you some immediate ideas and direction. The aim of these suggestions are to shift you from negativity to positivity.

Chapter 3

How to feel like you're enough and to accept who you are

The moment I decided to accept who I was, warts and all, was the moment my life changed. Finally, I surrendered and decided I was already enough and had nothing to prove to anyone else. I was done with constantly striving to be and do more and relentlessly chasing my dream life. I was never fully present and able to enjoy the moment, and this led to a constant feeling of discontent. I just wanted to enjoy my life again, appreciating fully the beauty around me, the people I cared about and being back in that place of trusting that everything is happening exactly as it was meant to. It was something I had not felt for a long time. Somewhere inside of me, I just knew I was on a journey of discovery, growth and change and this would last my entire lifetime.

I finally let go of the need to be anyone other than who I was, and to stop the comparing and competing. I was okay with who I was, where I was and I finally trusted that everything was unfolding perfectly for me. It was such a relief, to take off this heavy burden of needing to be something more, or different to who I was. Up until this point I was living with a constant fear and anxiety of being judged by others and coming up short. When I decided to let it all go, I suddenly had nothing to prove to anyone, least of all myself. I could just enjoy my own company again, embrace the present moment and just be.

Too often other people make us feel bad for what we want, what we need, who we are and how we live our lives. If we're not careful they can plant seeds of doubt in our mind. In truth, there's something about who we are and how we have chosen to live life that triggers them and makes them uncomfortable. Either they don't agree with our choices, we aren't behaving in the way they want us to, or we're drawing attention to areas of their life where they aren't happy and fulfilled.

Some of the more toxic people in your life may even be worried about how your own self-acceptance and the courage to live life with conviction, is going to impact them. Maybe you'll no longer be at their beck and call, or you won't be so desperate for their approval. This changes the dynamics of the relationship and makes them nervous, because potentially it threatens the chances of their needs being met.

A personal example of this is my strong need for alone time. Being a highly sensitive person (HSP) I need time alone and away from other people. I can often sense their emotions and their energy, and this is very tiring for me. As I opened up to my intuitive gifts and embraced energy more and more, I found I couldn't be around certain people for too long and excessive noise, crowds and stimulus was just too much for my nervous system. This is when I started declining social invitations. A few years ago I would have worried that I was being anti-social and I would have told myself that I should make more of an effort. Today, I know my choices are self-honouring and I'm always very open and honest with people about this.

I fully accept that sometimes people won't understand, my choices and I'm 100% okay with that. I commit to making conscious and aligned choices every day and to do what makes me feel happy, fulfilled and reenergised, and not fulfil an obligation or expectation. I would also rather spend quality time with fewer people who light me up and inspire me, than waste time with lots of people where we make small talk and where the environment drains me. This is not me judging anyone else, it's about me having a self-awareness of what I need.

It's such a shame that it took so long to reach this point, especially as I reflect on all the times I exposed myself to people and situations that really weren't nourishing my soul. I do however believe in divine timing and intervention and so maybe I still had lessons to learn.

Many of my clients are also sensitive souls and over stimulation through crowds, noise, smells etc can really impact their nervous system too. It's truly exhausting and despite their preference to avoid these situations, they often tell me they can't let their friends down and that they wouldn't understand. Ask yourself this, are they really your friend if they can't accept a fundamental part of who you are and what you need?

Self-acceptance is not always easy because you've had years of conditioning in your subconscious mind. There will even be days where you feel like you're going backwards. Where you once accepted and honoured who you are and your choices, someone has made you question yourself again. Stay strong and have the courage and conviction in yourself and your choices. Your own self-acceptance will make such a difference to so many areas of your life; more happiness, confidence, less stress and anxiety, feeling lighter, having better physical health and much better sleep.

If you're serious about choosing to be happy, you must accept who you are and what you desire and need. It's not about anyone else and what they think, how they choose to live their life, or about what you've been led to believe…it's about you. This is the perfect moment to give yourself permission to just be you. No need for improvements or fixing so that you can become slimmer, fitter, smarter and richer. Can you imagine what it would feel like to simply surrender and give yourself permission to love yourself exactly as you are and where you are?

I have worked with hundreds of women where self-acceptance is a huge challenge. Until they can accept themselves and where they are in life, it can be very hard for them to engage in self-care or to have any self-compassion. It's like they're trying to punish themselves by denying pleasure, until they feel they have earnt it, or deserve it. Take Sara, who was always striving to be more in her life and in her business. She would push away the opportunities to have fun, to laugh and to really enjoy life. She didn't feel like she deserved to stop and rest until her business had become more profitable. She was also denying herself fun and pleasure. It was exhausting for her and the harder she worked, the further away she pushed fun, laughter and pleasure, until one day she wondered what the point was to it all.

The journey to self-love and acceptance is a very personal thing and can affect each of us in many different ways, but in order to choose happiness we have choose self-acceptance and we have to reconnect with inner truth. I know there are time when you're so disconnected from how you feel, and you have all this inner conflict between the excitement of what life could be like and the fear of what it's going to take to make it happen. You've spent years wearing the perfect mask to cover up how you feel and to protect yourself from the outside world. The trouble is this mask is now blocking you from connecting with yourself.

I also know you've reached a point where you no longer trust yourself and this makes things much harder at times. You want to throw caution to the wind and just accept your intuition and commit to creating a better life, but that inner voice keeps shouting *'it's not safe, you'll never survive'*. You're judging yourself for being so weak and not having the strength to do what you need, but at times you feel frozen with fear or indecision. You're not alone with feeling like this. So many women have deeply ingrained beliefs, and they can stem from a lifetime of believing that you're not enough.

When we spend our time rejecting the parts of us that we deem as bad, wrong or not enough, it has a profound impact on how we live our life and more importantly our emotional, physical and spiritual health. A lack of self-acceptance, compassion and a low self-esteem, affects every choice and decision you make. Over time it can cause you to put up a wall around your heart to protect you from feeling emotional pain. This is a very effective technique as it really does block out all those horrid and painful emotions, but it also blocks your ability to feel all those amazing emotions too, such as love, joy, elation, contentment and pure peace. It's a huge price to pay.

Underneath the belief of not being acceptable, is a deep desire to know that you're okay, that you're loveable and worthy of love. Many of my clients seek this deep need for reassurance from others and yet they are not able to give this gift of acceptance to themselves.

They have given their power away by looking for someone, or something outside of themselves for validation of their self-worth and value. It's a dangerous game to play, because no matter how much external recognition they get, it will never be enough. Like an addict, they will come to rely on it and need an even bigger fix. If they don't get their fix, or what they need, the impact can be devastating. They've opened themselves up to a whole heap of pain. It's why self-acceptance is fundamental in living a happier life.

One of my clients Karen, was a high flying lady who worked in London and in a profession mainly dominated by men and yet on nearly every call, she would ask me if she was normal and if it was possible to help her when it came to her love life. Karen, like so many other women I have worked with, just wanted to know that she was enough as she was and that she wasn't flawed in some way. She valued adventure, excitement, travel and change. The exact opposite of all her female friends and because of this she thought there was something wrong with her. Please don't wait for someone else to give you permission to accept yourself, because you could be waiting forever.

Self-acceptance is the foundation of every relationship you'll ever have and how you treat yourself, sets the tone for how others will treat you too. It's time for you to be your own best friend. To extend the compassion, understanding and non-judgement that we usually only give to others. We need to begin seeing ourselves through the eyes of others and not through our own distorted lens.

If you're reading this book and you resonate with my energy, then let me assure you of this, you were not born to simply fit in, to be average, and to go unnoticed. You were meant to live an extraordinary life.

Exercise

I'm sure you've already begun to notice areas of your life where you need to gain more self-acceptance and where you need to be kinder to yourself. In the following exercise, I want to help you understand where you're not accepting who you are, before we then move onto understanding what's behind your actions and thoughts.

A powerful thing you could do, is work through this with a trusted friend or someone who knows you well. They can often spot things within your language and actions that you can't. Just remember to be open and curious about anything they share. There's no need to justify or defend, this is purely fact finding. The things that trigger you the most are likely to be the areas where you need to focus your attention, so be thankful for the gift of insight and their willingness to be open and honest.

Look through the following list of examples and just notice which ones feel very true for you. You may find awareness comes very quickly as to why you feel a certain way, or make certain choices, but don't worry if they don't. This will all come together in the rest of the book. It's why I always ask you to capture your insights in your journal, so you can always go back and review key insights and begin making important connections yourself.

- Your inner voice is very critical of everything you do and who you are. You constantly pick holes in how you look, how you dress, how you do your work, and the choices you make. It's relentless and it extends to all areas of life.

- You tell yourself that you can't do things. You fear you don't have enough ability or skill and that action will only lead to failure.

- You focus on all the reasons you shouldn't do something. Usually there is an underlying fear about the judgement and opinions of others. You're choosing to fit in and belong, or to avoid criticism and judgement instead of doing what feels right for you. At times you're filled with worry and anxiety over what other people may be saying or thinking about you.

- There are certain parts of yourself that you just can't accept, and you work hard to ensure that no one ever sees this part of you. You're scared that if they knew who you really were or what you were like, they might judge or reject you. You're pretending to be someone you're not and you're wearing a mask when it comes to your emotions.

- You're constantly comparing yourself to others and coming up short, even when you may not agree with their choices, or even want to be like them.

- You struggle to accept where you are in life right now, because life has not met your expectations. You're holding on so tightly to what you think life should look like and really you need to let go. You also just can't accept the part you played in reaching this point. We'll be diving deeper into this later in the book on the chapter about letting go.

- You constantly think about all the decisions and choices you've made and you wonder what you could have been thinking. You believe that other people make bad judgements and mistakes, but not you, you should have known better and chosen better. With this comes enormous guilt too, especially if your choices and decisions have impacted other people.

- You can be overly defensive, which is actually a self-protection mechanism, because you fear being attached. For example, when someone criticises or judges you, you're quick to lash out and become defensive and angry. Part of you is scared that what they have said is true and it's too painful to contemplate. Plus, you want the conversation to be over immediately and aggression can be an effective way of shutting people down.

- You're very critical of others. Attacking others is always easier than self-reflection and accepting decisions and choices you've made. If you direct everyone else's attention towards others, perhaps they won't look at you. It's the classic trick of illusionists, diversion of attention.

- Physically you may feel frustration, tension or anxiety. You can also feel tired, because you can be prone to over achievement, perfectionism and people pleasing. We'll be exploring all of these topics later in the chapter.

- You experience strong emotions such as hate, anger and resentment. Sometimes we direct this towards others and go into victim or blame mode.

- You feel apathetic and hopelessness, because you believe nothing will ever change, so what's the point.

- If you find yourself to be excessively controlling, pushy and always making others feel like they need to do and be more, then perhaps you need to look at what aspect within yourself you have decided is not enough.

The impact of all of the things above, is that you're not choosing happiness and you've closed down your heart to protect yourself from experiencing any more hurt and pain in your life. You may even have convinced yourself that you don't deserve more than what you have, whether this is love, money, success or happiness. You are enough and you do deserve to be happy.

Exercise

Now that you have a better understanding of what a lack of self-acceptance can look like, I want to go a little deeper and ask some more probing questions of you. This will deepen your self-awareness around this topic, and it will help you to identify your own personal triggers. Again, make sure you set some time aside to really reflect on these questions and if you can, do it with someone you trust. Having support and accountability, will encourage you to complete the exercise, and fully commit to your own self development. If you choose to be truthful and honest, the answers will be so enlightening, and I have no doubt they will allow you to transform yourself and your life in amazing ways.

Thinking about the examples I shared above and what you already know about yourself, answer the following questions:

1. Are there parts of yourself that you find hard to accept? This could be things such as; your physical appearance, something connected to your personality, the way you look at the world, something that you do, or the way you live your life. There really is no limit on this, just write down whatever comes up and refer back to the examples I shared if it helps.
2. Do you look to others, to validate that you're acceptable, loveable and enough as you are? For example, you may need your partner to tell you every day that they love you, or you'll doubt yourself. Or perhaps when it comes to work you need constant

positive feedback from clients, without this you suddenly slip into thinking you're useless, not as good as other people and that your clients hate you. I'm not exaggerating with this, I have many clients who genuinely feel like this. Think about who's validation you need and what you need from them?
3. Imagine that you would never get the external validation you need? What would this stop you from doing or being? Who does this impact, other than you?
4. What would need to happen, or be in place for you to be able to fully accept yourself? For example, if you found it hard to accept your body, you might say, 'I hate that I am overweight', then acceptance might be committing to a healthy diet and regular exercise.
5. Thinking about the previous question, why are those things so important to you? For example, the weight might be an issue because, all your friends are slim, fit and healthy and you don't like being the odd one out.
6. What has happened in the past that made you doubt your value or worth? In complete honesty, ask yourself if you've dealt with all the negative emotions connected to this?
7. Do you ever compare yourself to others? If so who in particular and why? What do they have that you want? Does this tell you anything about yourself?

I really admire you for taking the time to go through these questions and in being completely honest with yourself. Nothing in your life will change until you do, because everything starts from within. Although it's not always easy to face the truth, know that within the truth, there is also power. You've discovered so much valuable information about yourself; why you behave the way you do and why you make the choices and decisions that you do. At the end of this chapter, I'll share some practical tips that you implement straight away.

With your increased awareness of self-acceptance, we're now going to look at some key topics within this, people pleasing and perfectionism. Most people who struggle to accept themselves, display these traits, so it's an important area to explore.

Your need to be perfect is exhausting you

More and more women are falling prey to this need to be perfect and not only is it exhausting, it's taking us further away from who we really and from happiness. We're not allowing ourselves to stop and just enjoy the present moment, because everything on our to do list is not ticked off yet. We've decided that things in our life are not yet perfect enough and we're not perfect enough. It's impossible to choose happiness, when you're always striving for something. Your mind will constantly convince you that you'll only be happy, safe and enough when you've reached that next milestone, or when you and everything around you is perfect.

This need to push our bodies and minds to the absolute limit and to take on more than we really should, is because we genuinely don't believe we're enough as we are. We're lacking self-acceptance and we're trying to prove something. The trouble is, until we heal the emotional pain of this in our heart, nothing we do will ever be enough. Our achievements will feel empty and meaningless and instead of celebrating and rejoicing, we'll already be thinking about the next mountain we could climb, because maybe conquering that one will make us feel enough.

We have this strange belief that if we do more, achieve more and give more, then we'll be enough. We dream of our efforts being noticed by others, so that they finally realise just how amazing we are and begin to value us too. This gives us permission to stop and just enjoy life for a bit. Left to our own devices we will continue to push on, believing and fearing the worst about ourselves. The finish line just keeps moving and so the ache in our heart remains and the striving continues.

While technology and social media has been amazing at getting people all over the world connected, growing their businesses, getting educated and learning, it has also led to people feeling more disconnected from each other than ever. For the most part, people only share when things are going well, or they post what they want people to see. There is this huge pressure to keep up, to be perfect and as good as the next person. It's no surprise that anxiety and depression is on the rise and unfortunately the quick fix is often anti-depressants. While it helps initially, it doesn't solve the deeper problem and the inner work that is needed.

For many of us, we learned early in life that performing well, getting good grades, being good, being polite etc, all led to praise, attention and approval. Anything less than perfect was not acceptable and was met with criticism. This is crushing for a young child, who is still trying to find their place in the world. Ultimately what we are all seeking is approval for who we are, and to know we're enough and loveable as we are.

Anita is an amazing lady who has achieved so much through her business, but when I first met her she was very stressed, was on the edge of burn out and was over working all the time. She would readily admit it had impacted her marriage and she knew it stemmed from a childhood of feeling like she wasn't enough. She could never please her parents and they always demanded more of her. Looking back now, she can see it was because they saw her potential and wanted her to fulfil that. As a child who just wanted to be loved, she made it mean that nothing she did was enough and that she was not enough.

So many women go through life relying on achieving perfection to overcome that dreaded feeling of not being enough. They try and run from their fears of inadequacy towards approval, acceptance and praise. They are desperate to be free of anxiety, of being found out, of being humiliated in front of others and of simply not feeling as if they're enough.

Whether you associate with being an over achiever, or a perfectionist, you're engaging in a highly destructive habit, because you're always chasing and striving for something. Quite frankly it's exhausting, emotionally, physically and spiritually. These women are on a constant mission to prove to themselves and to others that they matter, that they're worthy of the space they take up, that they deserve to be seen and heard and that ultimately they deserve love. Whenever I come across women like this, I just want to hug them and wrap them up in love. I know the demons they're battling with, because they used to be mine too.

Overachieving and over giving, is actually a form of self-preservation. If we give more than people expect, then we believe we've done as much as we can to eliminate the risk of getting hurt and feeing like we aren't enough. We're doing everything we can to avoid criticism, judgement and the inner shame of not being enough in a world that demands so much. I love the author Brene Brown and these words ring so true for me; *'Perfectionism is a self-destructive and addictive belief system that fuels this primary thought: If I look perfect, and do everything perfectly, I can avoid or minimize the painful feelings of shame, judgment, and blame.... Research shows that perfectionism hampers success. In fact, it's often the path to depression, anxiety, addiction, and life paralysis'.*

As intelligent women, we know this quote is true, research proves it's true, but yet so many of us are stuck on that hamster wheel of pushing through pain, tiredness and emotional heartache. At all costs we must achieve more and we must be perfect. Why are we so attached to this? The answer is simple, because in childhood, with our innocent young view of the world, we formed the belief that achieving and being perfect was the only way to get attention, love and to stay safe. Our inner child is doing everything it can to survive, in the only way it knows how. Think back to the example of Anita, she knew that to get love and good attention and approval, she had to achieve top marks and be very successful. That's exactly what she did and what she strived for every day for years.

It's also important to remember that belonging, fitting in and being accepted is another of our most basic human needs and for some people they fear that being less than perfect could threaten this and their very survival. We decided that being perfect was the best way to stay safe and avoid emotional pain and exclusion.

The need to be perfect is something close to my own heart, because I always felt like I was trying to prove that I was enough to my dad. I figured that if I was the perfect child and did well at school, that perhaps he might like me and want to spend time with me. He might even become interested in who I was and my hopes and dreams. As an adult I know now that it wouldn't have mattered what I did or how perfect I was, but back then my thinking seemed to make sense.

I was also exceptionally close to my granddad and he loved hearing how well I was doing. I was the first in the family to go to University and travel the world and I topped this off by managing a big team in a financial organisation by the age of twenty-two and he couldn't have been prouder. Even then I associated achieving and doing things as a way to get attention and praise and be loved. If I wasn't being perfect, achieving or doing, then I risked feeling loved and I couldn't give that up. Leaving my corporate job and becoming a business owner was a total shock to the system, so many gremlins came to the surface, but that's a whole other story and book.

Can you see how easy it is to make a decision in childhood that can affect you forever, if you let it. These decisions can have a lasting impact not only on our sense of self, but also on friendships and relationships, especially if you don't recognise what you're doing and why. It can lead you to over giving, until you literally have nothing left. You will push yourself to give more and more to make the other person happy, despite the impact on you. Unfortunately, there are many toxic people out there, who will manipulate this trait and you. They will keep on taking and keep on demanding more from you, not caring that it's breaking your spirit and making you unhappy.

Perfectionism and over achieving are habits that have often been with us since childhood and it's not something that's easy to let go. It can take time to overcome this and to finally accept that we're already enough and have always been enough. We might question who we would we be without all this drive and who would we be if we weren't striving or doing.

Does any of what I've shared resonate for you? Can you see where this habit has snuck it's way into your life? If so, I want to help you understand what is going on within you and identify where a change in belief is needed.

Exercise

First of all, I'm going to share some examples of people who have traits of perfectionism, overachieving and over giving. As before, reflect on what feels true for you and what you identify with, work with someone else if you can and want to, and capture any insights in your journal. We'll then move onto some questions for deeper reflection on this topic.

- You find it very hard to just stop, rest and be. In those moments you can't define what you are doing, and it makes you uncomfortable, even guilty because surely you should be doing something.

- You continue working and pushing through, even when you're ill and really should be stopping.

- You struggle to ask for and accept help.

- Delegating is very hard for you. Firstly, you have to accept that you can't do it all alone and need help. Secondly, you have to let go of control and trust that someone will do it as well as you and you have to trust that they'll do it in a time scale that meets your approval.

- You take on too much, which is also connected with our boundaries, because it's so hard for you to say no and admit you can't do everything. You find yourself taking on too much and then you experience feelings of anger and resentment.

- You set yourself impossible standards. You live with constant pressure to do and be more.

- You put off starting something, because you fear failing and or not doing it well enough. This book is a great example of this, I started this book over three years ago and had a first draft done within eight weeks, but it took me two years to do all the editing, because I didn't want anyone else to see it until it was perfect. I didn't want my writing abilities to let me down, when the content was so important to me.

- You're very focused on the outcome of things. When things go well, or they are a success, you feel like this is a reflection of you

- If someone has given you a task, you'll always look at ways to over deliver and go above and beyond.

- You secretly fear you're not good enough and being criticised is very painful for you. You may even go into attack mode.

- You love and need feedback; it validates who you are.

- As soon as you finish one task or project, you're already thinking about the next thing to complete.

- You're always striving to have the perfect body, perfectly tidy house, perfect life, be a perfect wife etc. If you feel like you're failing in even one area, you jump to the conclusion that you're a failure and failing in all of life.

- You can be highly critical of others, thinking things such as *'they're so lazy'*, *'have you seen the state of their house'*, *'what do they do all day'*.

As you already know, over achievement and perfectionism is simply a choice we made to protect our younger self. When we can recognise where it came from and own that, we can then begin the process of choosing differently and releasing it. Now that you have an understanding of some of the traits of perfectionism and overachieving, let's go one-step further and see how this applies to you.

Answer the following questions and don't be surprised if some of the answers overlap what you identified about yourself in the first section of this chapter. Those confirmations show us that inner work is needed.

1. Can you identify areas of your life, where over achievement and perfectionism has gotten out of control?
2. How is perfectionism and overachieving keeping you safe?
3. Can you identify what people or situations make this habit worse for you?
4. What has been the impact on you emotionally and physically?
5. If you don't get this under control, how will it affect your life in the future and who else will it impact? Are you okay with this?
6. Whose approval, acceptance, attention and love were you, or are you, really after?

7. How would life look for you, if you dropped the need to be perfect? What would you let go of if you finally had nothing to prove?
8. Do you feel ready to let this go? If not, why not?

I know it might seem as if there are lots of things coming up for you right now and that perhaps you've opened a can of worms, but trust me, it's all part of the process. In order to choose happiness and to stay happy we have to understand our blocks to allowing this to happen. Keep reflecting, keep noticing how you feel and keep journaling. We'll talk about ways to deal with all of this later.

Stop allowing people to overstep your boundaries

Choosing to be happy can be impossible when we feel like other people are constantly overstepping our boundaries. We feel violated, exploited and far from happy. Instead we're dealing with anger, frustration and resentment and we're so mad at ourselves too for being such a push over.

Those that have low self-esteem and question their self-worth, often have a dysfunctional relationship with others. They tolerate behaviour that most people would not, because they feel they have no other choice, or they're not worthy of being treated any better. There is a constant fear of rejection, conflict or judgement. To set boundaries feels unsafe, because then they have to be honest and ask for what they want. They have no idea how the other person is going to respond, and this feel very unsettling. It feels easier to stay quiet, compromise yourself and conform, despite it making you desperately unhappy.

Exploring and knowing your boundaries is a significant part of being happy, because when you get this right, it will make a big difference to your relationships and how you feel. You'll feel accepted for who you really are and not what the other person wants you to do, You'll know they have your best interests at heart and you'll no longer have to carry emotions such as resentment, anger and a feeling of being insignificant. This puts you on the path to claiming back your personal power and increasing your self-esteem and own self-acceptance.

It's worth mentioning here that when you begin to enforce your boundaries and you start making yourself a priority, some people will push back and test you. You may hear comments such as; *'You've changed'*, *'I don't like who you have become'*, *'Why are you being so selfish?'*, *'Why don't you care?'* These people are trying to restore the previous dynamic in the relationship, one where they were in control and had power over you. Suddenly they feel very unsure of the relationships, because the rules have changed. Where they were once able to emotionally dump on you, rely on your constant support, or get you to do what they wanted, they're now faced with your resistance and they don't like this.

Remember their comments are not really about you. It's about where they're at in life and the deeper needs they're trying to meet. You may find that when you choose to honour and respect yourself, you're no longer a match for some people and so they will naturally remove themselves from your life. This brings a nice natural closure to things, so don't resist this change, because it's like trying to change the flow of a river. On this journey there will be friends who become strangers and strangers who become friends, embrace and accept that. The same is true for family, you may need to create distance from certain family members, because the relationship has become toxic for you. Always listen to your body, because it will tell you everything you need to know. Don't allow your logical mind to overrule what you feel.

Put very simply, boundaries are your rules and you can't expect other people to follow your rules, if you're unclear on them yourself. Just as players of a game know the rules before they engage on the field, you too must know your rules and also be prepared to share them with others in your life. Constantly complaining that others aren't treating you with respect, but never dealing with the issue, is simply choosing to be a victim. Get clear on your boundaries, lovingly enforce your boundaries and you'll feel much happier.

It's why getting to know yourself is so important. You have to get really clear on what your values are, what matters to you and what is acceptable behaviour and what are your absolute non-negotiables with people. This can take time and is something that lots of people struggle with, especially when they have been conforming, people pleasing and putting other people first for so long. Don't worry if this takes a bit of time and practice.

Let me bring this to life a little with my own example. My non-negotiables within a relationship or a friendship are honesty and loyalty. Betray me and I'll never trust you again and you'll never have my heart, or my loyalty. If someone breaches these things, I know the only option for me is to walk away or create distance, because feeling emotionally safe and secure matters to me more than anything. While I am good at forgiving, I never forget what someone is capable of.

Can you see how clarity and communication around boundaries is essential for you to have healthy relationships with people, both in your personal life and through your work. If you're unclear or have loose boundaries, you may find that people are constantly overstepping the mark with you. It would be easy to put all the blame on the other person, but if you're not clear yourself and you don't let the other person know when they've overstepped the mark, how can they show you the respect you deserve.

To help you understand boundaries a little more, I'm going to share the three most common boundaries. As we go through this section, just notice if any of these resonate for you. It could be the first time you've ever considered these things, so don't worry if you need some time to process before moving onto the questions in the exercise.

Physical boundaries

Physical boundaries are everything connected to your own body, your home, your possessions. You always get to choose how close people can come to you, who can touch you and how, who is allowed into your home and what they're allowed to do when they're there. This isn't about you being overly precious, it's about asking other people to respect what is physically yours.

For those who are sensitive souls, I'm going to take this one step further, because a physical boundary for me is refusing to be around people who moan and complain all the time. The energy of these people can often feel like an energetic assault on my body. I literally feel like I'm shrinking and my very life force is being sucked out of me. It doesn't matter who these people are, family members, colleagues or close friends, you do not have to spend time with them or allow this.

Taking this to the extreme, physical boundaries is also about protecting your body from harm. For some people it means leaving an abusive relationship or situation.

Emotional boundaries

Having emotional boundaries, means that you hold the right to have and experience your own emotions and feelings, without being made to feel wrong for them. Sometimes there is no clear or logical reason why you feel the way you do and it's not for anyone else to tell you that you're wrong. No one else has lived your life or truly knows what you know, so you have the right to feel however you want to feel. If this negatively impacts them in anyway, they always have the choice to lovingly enforce their own boundaries and choose not to spend time with you.

Having strong emotional boundaries, also prevents you from taking on other people's blame, guilt and general negativity. It's very common for people to lash out at others, especially when they're struggling to deal with their own feelings and emotions and don't want to take responsibility for their life and choices. When you're strong within yourself, you can literally let their negativity and comments bounce right off you.

Finally, there is no need for you to take on responsibility for other people's problems. It's okay to be concerned and supportive, but it's not your job to fix, save or rescue them. It doesn't matter who they are, our family, our partners, our friends, they all have their own path to walk and when we try and carry all of their burdens, not only are we enabling the behaviour, we are depriving them of the chance to learn and grow.

This last boundary is especially true if you're used to over giving and you're in a caring profession. The lines here can get so blurred. We want those in our life to be happy, successful, healthy and free from emotional pain, but, if we allow ourselves to carry the responsibility for all this, some of those people will abuse you. They'll expect you to fix them, save them and rescue them, time and time again, thereby giving away their own power. Eventually, you'll find yourself increasingly resentful, angry and exhausted.

Mental boundaries

To have strong mental boundaries, means that you feel confident to stand by your own thoughts, values and opinions, and don't feel the need to have others agree with you. As you can imagine, this is such a challenging boundary for some people, as the thought of speaking their truth and dealing with conflict is terrifying.

Having strong mental boundaries, is knowing you don't need to have the same viewpoint as everyone else and that it's okay to disagree. Just look at the world around us, it would never have developed as fast, if some people weren't willing to hold fast to their own views. Without their inner resolve, they would not have been able to bring certain things to the world, just think of modern-day geniuses, like Steve Jobs, Elon Musk or Richard Branson.

Do my boundaries need tightening up?

There's been a lot to think about so far and I bet you're already thinking about some of the people in your life and what's happened in the past. You're probably even reflecting over the way you've handled certain situations and how it made you feel. All of this reflection will help you to know if you need to tighten up your boundaries, because when you look back, you'll feel some of those more negative emotions; anger, resentment, anxiety, betrayal, disappointment and maybe things like shame and humiliation.

Don't worry if nothing is coming to mind at the moment. You can always get clear on your boundaries, by simply experiencing life and paying attention to how you feel in the present moment. You'll soon become aware of any breaches in boundaries. For example, the next time you're with someone and you can feel anxiety, anger, resentment or a shift in your energy, consider what is going on. There's a good chance that they've overstepped your boundaries, so ask yourself why.

Exercise

Now that you have a better understanding of boundaries and what it can relate to in your life, take some time to reflect on the following questions. Don't feel like you have to answer these all in one go, as you become willing to have clarity, more awareness will come. There is no rush and no race, do this in a way that means you complete the work and you don't fall into a state of overwhelm. It took years to shape your life and it can sometimes take just as long to unpick things. Answer the following questions and make sure you capture any insights in your journal:

1. Are there people in your life that are doing or saying things, that don't sit well with you? Can you identify why this doesn't feel right or good for you?
2. Do you know what is, and isn't acceptable from someone you spend time with?
3. Are people using you as their emotional dumping ground?
4. Have people overstepped your boundaries in terms of what they are discussing or expressing? This can include things like, political views, animal welfare, parenting, religion, money or sex.
5. Are you being asked to act outside of your values?
6. Are you putting the needs of others first?
7. Is there a concern that if you asserted your boundaries that the relationships would break down?
8. Are there people that you need to spend less time with?

A big part of setting boundaries and lovingly enforcing them is knowing that you deserve more and are worthy of more. There is nothing more you need to do and you're already enough. If any of these fears or beliefs keep popping up for you, then you know more exploration and healing needs to be done in these areas. We have already looked at limiting beliefs and the chapter on fear is next, so within this book you'll have all the resources you need to master this.

As your understanding and awareness of boundaries grows, I suspect that you'll want to make some big changes in some areas of your life. Taking steps to put these changes into place will have a knock on affect; you'll feel better about yourself, you'll know yourself in a deeper way, your physical health will improve and you'll find that the people you choose to spend time with, are more inspiring and uplifting. At the end of the following section, I'll share some advice in terms of how to set and enforce loving boundaries, but first onto people pleasing.

Are you a recovering people pleaser?

Many of my clients will often say that they have people pleasing tendencies, or that like me, they're a recovering people pleaser. Of all the habits I wanted to personally break, this one was the most challenging for me. If you're a people pleaser too, then you'll know that this habit is exhausting. Your life is about making sure other people are happy. For some reason you've come to believe that everyone else's happiness is more important than your own and this puts you in a position of constantly giving.

In those moments we're not speaking up for ourselves, or even being ourselves. We're so worried what other people might think or say, that we decide it's easier to conform, avoid conflict and just do what pleases them. We contort ourselves into being someone that makes them more comfortable, just think about the woman who is so desperate to ensure that everyone around her is happy, that she puts her needs last. She becomes the daughter, wife, mother, sister and friend that those around her need her to be, what she thinks and what she needs doesn't even come into it.

The only trouble is, this is not who she is and so now she feels uncomfortable in her own skin. She is emotionally and physically exhausted, disconnected from her truth, her intuition and what she wants from life and she's begun to question herself at every turn. This is often when I hear clients say, *'I don't know who I am anymore'*.

Very often this then leads to anger, resentment, hurt and disappointment towards the very people you have been trying to please for so long. Every day you're walking on eggshells and waiting for the moment when you'll meet with their disapproval. You know that these people don't have your best interests at heart, and you should voice your truth, but you're so tired of not being heard and not getting your needs met that you've given up trying. You struggle to understand how someone who supposedly cares for you could treat you with such disregard and how you could have allowed yourself to tolerate it.

Some of you reading this book might think that people pleasing isn't a problem for you, but ask yourself if this is true of all people in your life. Sometimes we can have that one person, who constantly pushes our buttons and makes us behave in ways even we struggle to understand.

Take Beth for example, she was exceptionally strong and very forthright with everyone in her life, apart from her mother and her husband. Both of these people brought out the people pleaser in her and she was often a doormat for both of them. For Beth it was about keeping the peace and not having to deal with conflict in the home. Growing up life was very unstable and uncertain, with lots of drama, conflict and stress. As an adult she was doing whatever was necessary to avoid this, even though this meant a constant breach of her boundaries, being emotionally manipulated and emotionally abused.

Let me share some examples of how people pleasing could be playing out in your life right now, before we then look at why you choose to engage in this behaviour.

- You say yes to people because, you feel bad letting someone down and disappointing them.

- You say yes to something, even though you don't really want to do it and it's not convenient for you.

- You take on too much work, or responsibility for everything and everyone in your life. You're often swooping in to save people, or sort things out.

- You really want to do or say something, but you hold yourself back, because you know the other person is not going to like it and you're unsure how they could react.

- When in discussions or arguments, you don't stand up for yourself, even when you know you're in the right. It's easier and at times safer to agree, because potential conflict feels very unsafe.

Saying no and speaking our truth, is a key part of having healthy boundaries and living a happy and content life. Just remember this quote, '*No uttered from the deepest conviction is better than a yes merely uttered to please, or worse, to avoid trouble."* Mahatma Gandhi.

Let's explore why you might be fearful of expressing your true feelings and why you people please. As always record your insights and thoughts in your journal.

- You have a fear of judgement, rejection and criticism.

- You want to be accepted, belong and fit in. Being abandoned terrifies you.

- Staying safe and experiencing peace is your top priority. You do everything you can to avoid conflict and arguments.

- You question if you deserve happiness or more from life, so you put others first. There is a deep sense of responsibility for others and so you must do everything you can to make sure they're happy.

- You worry that people won't like you; this triggers old wounds of not being enough and not being lovable.

- When it comes to work or business, you may fear losing a client or the money it would bring.

- For those people who are highly sensitive, there is even more pressure to people please, because you can literally feel what the other person wants you to do and say. Plus, you can feel the disappointment and anger when they aren't getting their needs met. It feels like being winded and so you choose to conform.

When you can identify what you're trying to protect yourself from, it's easier to become free. You understand the deeper physiological needs that your inner child is trying to meet, and as an adult you can take action to ensure she feels safe. Just remember, how you feel about yourself is ultimately more important than other people's views and opinions. If you wait around for the approval of other people before you truly accept yourself, or live your ideal life, you could end up missing some truly magical moments.

Exercise

Now that you understand what people pleasing could look like and why you might do this, it's time to answer some questions. Having a greater understanding and awareness of your people pleasing is going to transform your relationships and lead to deeper and more genuine connections with people. If this sounds like exactly the sort of thing you're missing at the moment and you feel ready to find your voice and to be brave, answer the following questions and then I'll share some useful tips and tools to bring this whole chapter together.

1. Do you ever find yourself saying yes to people, when you really want to say no? What does this tend to happen with? Who does this tend to happen with? Ask yourself what you're try to achieve with this person, or what you're afraid of?
2. Are you agreeing with something because it feels safer or easier than dealing with conflict, drama and uncertainty?

3. In order to break this habit, are there people that you need to spend less time with?

The questions and answers on your boundaries and people pleasing, are likely to overlap and complement one another. This is to be expected, because these two areas go hand in hand. We allow our boundaries to be breached, because we are a people pleaser.

The following are some final tips on how to improve your levels of self-acceptance, lovingly assert your boundaries and to stop people pleasing. Make a note in your journal about any that you would like to commit to:

- I love to get curious about my emotions, because I believe they're trying to get my attention and tell me something. Rather than judging myself, I prefer to see these emotions as an opportunity to learn more about where I need more alignment in my life, or where I need to do some more inner healing. Stop and listen to what your emotions are trying to tell you.

- Accept how you feel, even when the emotions are negative. Don't fight against what is and don't get annoyed with yourself, thinking you're a bad person. Embrace those feelings of anger, disappointment or failure, because in the moment, that is how you feel. It doesn't mean you have to lash out, or act irrationally, it's purely about acceptance and then a positive release. It will help you to heal at a much deeper level and make lasting changes.

- Express gratitude for the fact that every decision you have made has brought you to this point and made you who you are. Without those decisions perhaps you wouldn't have your partner, your family, your pets, your friends, your job or your home.

- Recognise that you may need to forgive yourself and release the old emotions. There is no need to carry shame, guilt or regret anymore. We'll be looking at self-forgiveness later in the book. If this feel relevant for you, make a note in your journal about anything that is present for you now and know we'll come back to this.

- Use energy shifting modalities such as meditation, EFT/Tapping, energy work such as reiki, and breath work. The key thing here is that the modality resonates for you and that you trust the practitioner if you're choosing to be supported.

- Get clear on what your boundaries are and what is and is not acceptable for you. This may take some time, especially if you have had a lifetime of people pleasing. Working through the questions in this chapter, will help with this.

- Make a list of your boundaries. For example, I do not want my mum to moan about my dad in front of me anymore, or when my friends ask which restaurant we should eat in, I am going to be honest and say where I really want to go.

- Think about how you could set your boundaries firmly and assertively, but from a place of love. Can you identify the things or people that are likely to challenge you and cause you to give in? Capture some ideas or ways of saying things so that you feel prepared. In times of stress, or when someone significant in your life challenges your boundaries, it will be very easy to give in. Consider the impact and emotional pain if you were to give in, this is likely to give you the courage to be firm.

- Set your boundaries from a place of love and not a place of anger. This is about respecting and honouring yourself, not about making a point to those in your life. It is about being calm, confident and assertive. If those around you push back, respond calmly and again set your boundary.

- Who in your life has great boundaries? What do they do or say? Having a role model is a great way to see first-hand how others deal with boundaries and more importantly how it impacts their life.

- Practice saying no and speaking up. It will feel uncomfortable at first, but think about the hours or days you can waste feeling resentful, versus a minute of discomfort in speaking your truth.

- Do you need to spend more time meeting your own needs? What can you start to do differently and who's support do you need?

- Play the no game. Every time someone asks you to do something, make your default answer no, even if this is just in your head and then reflect on whether you really want to do this. I used to have a tendency to offer support, say yes instantly or volunteer for things when I was already over committed. This gave me some space to think about whether I really wanted to do it, or whether I would end up saying yes and feeling resentful and angry.

There is lots to think about in this chapter, but there are some small things listed above that you can start doing today that would impact the quality of your life and build your confidence. I know that often fear of the unknown can take over and that's why in the next chapter, we'll be exploring fear.

Chapter 4

Fear creeps into all our lives

You want to choose happiness, but no one told you it was going to be so hard, so scary at times and was going to mean you had to be brave. As you've made your way through the last few chapters, I'm sure you've noticed lots of fear arising. Fear around the action you need to take, the changes that need to be made, or simply the fear that if you choose to do nothing, that nothing will ever change. Part of your mind has jumped into the future and played out all these different scenarios and is now in panic mode. Everything feels so overwhelming; where do you start, what do you focus on first, what if you fail, what is your priority? So many questions and these decisions are exactly what can keep you stuck and confused.

Fear is the voice in your head, which says, if you start making new decisions and taking action, you won't be able to cope with the change, life will become too unpredictable and that doesn't feel very comfortable or safe. This is especially true if you resonate with being a control freak and needing to have all the answers. In those moments you have a choice whether to stay safe and believe that voice in your head, or decide that now is the time to face your fears, embrace change and move forward in life.

When we commit to change and to ourselves, everything suddenly becomes exciting and life is full of possibilities. Even though part of us is enjoying the changes and we feel more aligned with our new life and choices, fear can still kick in. We begin to feel anxious, fearful and this is when the doubt can set in. We worry about all the things that might happen and it pulls us away from the joy of the present moment. Just know that what you're experiencing is simply fear. It's the part of you that is trying to keep you safe by avoiding all change and keeping life predictable. This fear is not real, it's simply the projections of your subconscious mind. A combination of learned behaviours and your personality formed from years of living life on other people's terms and carrying their fears within you.

Just as people are wide and varied, so too are fears and they affect each of us differently. One thing remains the same though, our fears keep us stuck and prevent us from having the life we really want. We choose to settle for less than we deserve because it feels more comfortable and at least we can predict how each day is going to turn out and this in part makes us feel in control and safe.

Let's look at the example of Ruth. She was desperate to make some big changes in her life. She knew what needed to be done, but she was scared to take action. The conversation she needed to have with her husband felt overwhelming. She needed more from her marriage and she was just not sure if her husband was capable of being the man she needed him to be. They had gone around in circles for years, Ruth expressing what she needed and her husband promising to change. She was tired of the constant disappointment and frustration and she made a decision that it was time to leave the marriage. She had all this fear about confronting him as she was fearful about how her husband would react, and how she would cope as a single woman with children.

Ruth knew she wasn't happy; she knew exactly what she needed to do in order to become happy and yet she sat with the fear of the future and her husband's reaction for years. It was such a waste of time and energy and yet the fear took over. She sacrificed years without the love she really craved and deserved, and her husband only ever had a shell of his wife, something that I'm sure he was more than aware of. I'm pleased to tell you that Ruth has since been very open and honest with her husband and they both agreed that separating was the best option for both of them. She now has her own house, a job she loves that gives her financial stability and an active social life. She finally chose happiness over fear.

Let's look at a list of fears that I see people dealing with every day. This list is only the tip of the iceberg, but it gives you an idea of what other people are struggling with and it lets you know that you're not alone. Fear of failure, fear of success, fear of rejection, fear of criticism, fear of not being enough, fear of public speaking, fear of change, fear of ending a relationship, fear of starting a relationship, fear of changing jobs, fear of specific things, for example, spiders or flying. The list really could go on and on and it includes very small fears, right up to those big fears which have a profound impact on our life.

If we let fear rule our lives, we are depriving ourselves of what it means to be truly alive. To experience joy, love, passion, happiness, success, connection and so much more. Do you really want to live a life where these things are not even a possibility for you? To live each day knowing that nothing more is possible seems totally soul destroying to me. One of the key things that gets me through the lows of life and the emotional struggles, is knowing that tomorrow is a new day and I can always choose differently. I'll never part with this optimism, because then I would be giving away my power and my dreams. I'm guessing you must feel the same or you wouldn't be reading this book.

You need to change how you look at fear, because as stated by Steve Pavlina, *'Fear is not your enemy. It is a compass pointing you to the areas where you need to grow'.* Often people feel afraid and anxious and naturally assume they're fearful or suffering with anxiety, but what if your anxiety and fear was simply telling you that you were currently out of alignment. That in truth, you were ready to grow and expand and that more was available to you. What if these feelings were your soul's way of getting your attention and asking you to wake up, embrace change and choose differently? Having this approach to fear is so empowering, it can potentially change everything for us.

For most people, fear is about feeling out of control, uncertain, anxious and very uncomfortable. Something to avoid at all costs if you can.

Physically, it starts with a feeling of panic and anxiety, which is closely followed by an increase in heart rate. Your breathing can become shallow and quick and you start to feel butterflies in your stomach. For some, fear is the start of adrenaline pumping through your body. You're ready for fight or flight, which is useful energy to harness if you have a real threat in front of you to deal with, but it's not healthy for your body if the response is simple down to dealing with an uncomfortable situation. When this response becomes a habit within us, it puts us on edge constantly. Just think about the people you know who seem to have a mass of nervous energy, there's a good chance that they're dealing with fear.

Emotionally, it's about not knowing the outcome and being afraid that you won't be able to cope or deal with what happens. We imagine the worst case scenario and our mind is tormented by worrying and repetitive thoughts. The whole process is exhausting. We can fear looking silly, being humiliated, not being heard, not getting the result or outcome we had hoped for, and so many other things.

This is why so many people choose to stay stuck and procrastinate. Even though their life is causing them pain, they know exactly what to expect each and every day. There is a strange comfort in that, and as the saying goes, better the devil you know.

We all know people like this. They're the ones who never seem to move forward in life. They bitch, moan and complain and yet will never take action. They're choosing to be a victim of life. For some it's because it meets a deeper psychological need within them and for others it's because fear has them in it's grasp. These are often those who have a strong dislike for their life and need to make changes the most. It's so clear to everyone around them, that they're definitely not choosing happiness.

Take a moment to recall the feelings you experienced from the earlier exercise, where you focused on the future and nothing changing in one, three, five, and ten years' time. If you need some time to reconnect with these emotions, repeat the exercise, or refer to your journal. When these feelings feel heavy, negative and repressive, then you know it's time to commit to change and face your fears.

Just remember, if you give into the fear and nothing changes, you'll wake up every day next to the same person, or to that same empty space beside you. You'll walk through the same day, with the same routine and same people in your life, causing you the same heartache and drama's. You'll experience the same emotions, fears, doubts and indecision and all of this will drain your energy and excitement of life. The way you feel about yourself will be no different, every curve you loath now, will still be there taunting you, every doubt you have about your worthiness to be, do or have more will still be present in your mind. Everything will be the same.

Allow yourself to fully imagine that future, walk through every part of that future. See it in your mind's eye, feel it with every part of your body, don't allow yourself to suppress anything. It's time to find the fire within you and to connect with what you really want from this life. I want you to commit to yourself and to begin taking action, so that you can make your desires a reality.

When I did this exercise I just knew that it was time to start acting fearlessly. No way was I waking up to the same life, I deserved more and I wanted more. I was sick of trying to be more and achieve more. I was tired of working so hard and yet not having the success I desired, or believed I deserved. I was exhausted at my lack of boundaries and of living my life to ensure other people were happy and had their needs met. I knew it was time to make myself a priority in my own life, because in that moment, I had nothing more to give anyone and it was all my own doing. My own fear of speaking up had created the life I was living and I was ready to say, I've had enough.

Consider the question you answered earlier in chapter one, *'What can I no longer tolerate in my life'*. Are you serious about the things you identified, did you mean it with your whole heart, or would it just be nice if things changed? The energy behind your intention has to be strong, or you'll never commit to seeing change through when it gets too hard, or when you can't see the solution. You'll choose to believe that there isn't a way out and that you'll just have to accept the life you're living, unless someone comes to rescue you.

Let me be really brutal and very clear, there is only one person who can change your reality and that's you. There is no knight in shining armour coming to save you, because this is your journey and your life is your responsibility.

I'm sure for some of you, this stirs up panic and brings you out in a cold sweat. You're already listening to all the old beliefs and stories in your mind about yourself, *'I can't do it'*, *'I'll never cope if I fail'*, *'I don't know enough'*, *'I don't have it in me'* and *'I can't do this alone'*. If these beliefs pop into your mind, don't fight them or judge them. Notice them and be curious about where they come from and why you have those beliefs. Write them down in your journal and remember that these are simply limiting beliefs, stories you have told yourself to prevent growth. You can revisit the earlier chapter and exercises on your mindset and limiting beliefs if you feel you still have some inner work to do.

The panic of knowing that your life is your responsibility, will also cause some of you to go into victim mode, you'll want to blame others for why your life looks this way and why you're suffering. The thought that you've created the life you're living is too much for you. Whatever your reaction, unless you decide that you're ready to take full responsibility for your life, to be courageous and to take action, then life is never going to change.

Blaming others for the reality you're currently dealing with is very disempowering. It can enforce the belief that you're powerless and have no control over things. This book is not only about helping you to see that you can choose to be happy, it's also a tool for helping you to see, or remember how powerful, brave and courageous you are. For me, it was incredibly powerful to take full responsibility for my life, because it meant that if I had created the life I was living, then I could choose again and choose a different reality. I didn't have to wait for permission, or outside events, or other people to shape my life.

Happiness is not reserved for some exclusive few. The happy people you aspire to be like, are no more special then you. It may just be that they've done the inner work to deal with their emotions and so it was easier for them to choose happiness. Don't allow your logical mind to trick you into thinking it was easy for them. I have no doubt that they, like me, had dark days, difficult conversations to navigate and times when they simply wanted the world to leave them alone. The difference is that they had a strong inner belief in what was possible for them and what they were capable of and this strengthened their ability to bounce back and keep moving forward.

You can have health, wealth and happiness just as they do, you just have to be prepared to take action and make it happen. You have to be brave and courageous and keep hold of that inner strength, knowing that every time you fall, you will get back up, you will brush yourself down and you will continue on your path. You only fail when you decide to stop trying.

So many people talk about wanting a better life. One that is full of love, joy, health and abundance, but you need to be honest with yourself and ask if you're truly ready to do what's necessary to make that happen. If you're pausing and doubting, ask yourself why. Jack Canfield says, *'Everything you want, is on the other side of fear'* and I couldn't agree more. Knowing that what you're feeling is fear, gives you such power, because you can finally see that it has nothing to do with your abilities, your knowledge, or how deserving you are. It's simply an emotion, that with the right tools, you can overcome.

Exercise

Take some time to answer the following questions, as this will help to establish how strong your inner motivation is for creating change and facing your fears. Make a note in your journal of the thoughts that arise:

1. Growth, change and expansion always happens beyond our comfort zones, are you willing to feel uncomfortable and to face your inner demons?
2. Even when you feel overwhelmed, confused and scared, are you willing to step outside of your comfort zone and take the necessary action to create your dream life?
3. When your inner voice makes you question what you're capable of and if you're enough, will you commit to yourself and leave behind the negative inner chat and the limiting beliefs?
4. When others in your life try and control and manipulate you, when they drain you of energy and enforce your negative thinking, will you willingly release those toxic people from your life and know that you can and will thrive without them?
5. Are you ready to believe that you make good decisions and that you're strong enough to cope with anything that life throws at you?

Don't judge yourself if you can still feel resistance within you, this is totally normal, and I would be lying if I said that every time I had a surge of positive energy I always pushed on. Sometimes I needed to take a breath and lean into the resistance too. If you can still feel fear, anxiety, overwhelm or panic, take a few minutes to check in with yourself and ask yourself these questions:

1. What fears are still present for me and still feel very real?
2. What are you worried might happen? Think about the scenarios you're playing out in your mind. Our imagination can be so powerful and creative, but we need to ensure it's working with us and not against us.
3. Are you trying to make the perfect choice and so you're waiting until you're 100% sure?
4. Why do you believe that you can't do something?
5. Are you scared about who you might become in the future and what this might mean for you?
6. Why does change feel so scary and overwhelming for you?
7. Is this triggering any feelings of being out of control? Many people need control to feel safe, they need clarity, they need predictability, they crave familiarity and they need all the answers.
8. Do you know what being in control means for you? What does it look like and feel like?
9. Do you already know what you want and need to do, and what action is required, yet you're choosing to procrastinate and putting things off?

Once you have more clarity on the above and you feel ready to move on, it's time to start exploring some of the most common fears that I help clients to deal with. I'll share some information about each fear and then I'll pose some insightful questions for you to reflect on. At the end of this chapter, I'll also share some practical tips that you can put into place immediately, or add to your action plan.

Remember I believe in you and I know you're capable of great things, because if I can create change in my life, so can you. It's time to start seeing that strength and power within yourself.

Fear of making the wrong decision

When we've forgotten how to trust ourselves and we're feeling disconnected from our own intuition, it can feel impossible to make a decision. We no longer trust the wisdom of our body and we no longer listen to the whispers of our heart and soul. Our logical mind and the part of us that is desperately trying to keep us safe takes over. If we could eliminate the fear of making the wrong decision, we could lessen the fear we feel. So much worry and anxiety is attached to choosing the wrong thing, the wrong path, or the wrong person.

Many of my clients come to their sessions confused by what decision they should make. They're terrified of making the wrong choice in their life or business. Not only are they worried about failing, or looking stupid, they're also worried about the time, energy and money they could waste by making the wrong choice. I would love to be able to make things easier for them and for you with my magic wand, but when it comes to making decisions, not all of them are logical.
What seems like the right and sensible thing to do, is not always the choice we're meant to make. Our decisions may not always make sense to other people and even to us at times, but when we feel confident, strong and connected to ourselves, we know without doubt that this is the right choice for us. We're prepared to take a leap of faith, because something within us just knows that this is the right thing to do. When it comes to making these types of decisions, we have to trust our intuition, and this means knowing ourselves at that deeper level and knowing how our intuition communicates with us.

Like most people, I have often delayed making decisions over the smallest of things as I weigh up all the facts, but when it comes to the houses I've lived in, I've always just known in an instant. I would literally see a picture and something within me said *'that's your home'*. I've never doubted these feelings and even when it looked like the buyers wouldn't sell to me, or the landlords were choosing another tenant, I never lost my faith and ploughed ahead as if it was happening. Even the threat of being homeless in a matter of days didn't deter me, which happened more than once I should add, once with children in tow. I had total belief and there was no space for fear. There are times when I wish I could replicate and bottle that sense of fearlessness, because it was just so strong within me. Working on trusting my intuition and myself, has made a massive difference to how I approach decision-making. It's not easy every time and I don't always get it right, but without exception, I learn more about myself and how my inner wisdom speaks to me.

I would love you to have a strong inner strength and a confident knowing about the choices you were making, because staying in indecision is a total waste of your time and energy. Just reflect back on a situation where you knew a decision had to be made and you wouldn't commit one way of the other. If you're like most people dealing with indecision, I expect the situation was swimming around your mind from the moment you woke up, until the moment you fell asleep. News flash, your subconscious mind was no doubt processing the entire time you were asleep too, which is why you woke up exhausted. Without that drain on your energy and time, just imagine what else you could have done, achieved and felt.

The inability to make a decision can cause us an immense amount of mental trauma. We flit back and forth between options and the emotional strain begins to take its toll. For some anxiety, depression, panic and fear become a normal part of life. This doesn't even take into consideration the physical stress that these emotions place on the body, adrenal fatigue, burnout, chronic fatigue syndrome, IBS and other digestive health challenges, headaches, back aches and so much more. If you knew that by making a decision that you could reduce or eliminate some of these things from your daily life, would you finally be ready to decide?

When you've spent years dealing with self-doubt, perfectionism and people pleasing and you're always fearful of being out of control or getting it wrong, making the right decisions can feel incredibly hard. Your mind is constantly creating scenarios where you made the wrong choice, where you failed, where you were rejected or ridiculed. It feels so real in our body and mind and in those moments, we're paralysed with fear and so we choose not to choose. Whether we accept it or not, this state of not choosing is in fact choosing to stay stuck, it's pure procrastination. We'll look at procrastination in more depth in a later chapter, but essentially this is all about putting something off which we know is good for us and is needed.

When you choose to do nothing, you have decided that taking responsibility for your own life and the direction it will take is too scary and unpredictable, and so in that moment you have chosen to stay stuck and to be powerlessness. Perhaps you think you won't be able to cope with what may happen, and so it feels easier and safer to do nothing. Maybe you even have a little moan to others about how cruel life is and how people are holding you back.

I know that was a little direct, but as you already know, I've been in this space myself before and I've also chosen not to make decisions when it came to some pretty important things in my life. I hoped that someone, or something would come along and save me and it never happened. It's like having money worries and buying a lottery ticket, thinking that will solve everything. You're coming from a place of powerlessness and you're choosing to believe that you don't have it within you, to change the course of your life. I believe that you do. You just need to get in touch with that side of yourself again and remember how powerful you can really be.

The fear of making the wrong decision is also why so make people seek outside counsel. Just think of all those people who consult tarot cards or psychics, friends and family before making a decision. They're giving their power away because they don't trust themselves and what they feel. They also know that taking action means facing challenges, dealing with difficult situations and pushing past their comfort zones, so consulting others is a great distraction. It's like embarking on a big fact-finding project. Plus, it gives them a handy person to blame if it doesn't work out well.

Don't get me wrong, I do enjoy having my cards read, but I would never base big life decisions upon the interpretation of cards, or the words of another. There are so many variables within this; how experienced is the person doing the reading, how much are they placing their own spin on things, are they projecting their own stuff onto you and the reading, are they having an off day, are they doing their own inner work so that they're a pure channel of love and light. You can see from these things alone how careful we need to be when giving our power away to someone outside of ourselves.

Would it make it easier for you to make decisions, if you knew that there were no wrong choices in life? I know that perfectionism will make it hard for you to accept that there are no wrong choices to be made, because you'll always want to look for the perfect decision. For now, pay attention to how your body and mind is responding to the thought of this. If you can already feel your body softening and wanting to relax, then it's fair to say this fear is very present and real for you. Perhaps go back and review the previous chapter on perfectionism and overachieving again before you move on. It's time to get really clear on how those emotional triggers and habits are affecting your ability to make decisions and what is really going on for you.

For now, what if you were to trust in something bigger than you and to accept that every decision was key and pivotal in your life's journey. Call it fate, destiny, god, divinity or source, whatever term best suits you, but because of this belief and inner knowing, you knew that you simply couldn't make a bad or wrong decision. You have complete faith that you'll always end up exactly where you're meant to be.

Exercise

Answer the following questions and ensure you capture any insights in your journal:

1. Do you trust yourself and your intuition? If not, why not?
2. Do you have an awareness of how your intuition communicates with you?
3. What scares you most about making the wrong decision?
4. Where are you giving your power away, and to who, when it comes to making decisions? Do you constantly ask everyone else's opinion about what to do?
5. Can you see where your indecision is impacting your emotional or physical well-being?
6. How would it feel to believe that all decisions were part of your life's plan? Every decision made you who you are today and has brought you to this very moment? It's okay to feel anger, resentment and injustice if life doesn't look the way you had hoped or expected. We'll be exploring how to reach a place of acceptance of what life looks like in the chapter on letting go. For now, just noticing and owning these emotions are key in your healing process.

Now that you have clarity over where this fear is holding you back when it comes to the fear of making the wrong decision, we're now going to explore the fears of judgement, rejection and criticism.

At the end of this chapter on fear, I'll share a number of practical tips and suggestions for you to implement. For now, let's just continue on with deepening your own self-awareness.

Fear of judgement, rejection and criticism

Some of the most common things I hear from people when it comes to fear of the future and the consequences of their actions, is the fear of judgement of others, rejection from those they care about and criticism for who they are and what they believe. It causes them to shrink and hide away in the shadows, pulling back from the world because they're scared to shine too brightly. They're scared to be seen and be truly visible, because they just feel so exposed and vulnerable.
Standing out to them means taking the risk that they could end up alone and this is a feeling that most people will try and avoid. Connection, community and belonging is part of the human experience, we want to be accepted and to fit in. We want to be unconditionally loved for who we are, but often we have witnessed, or experienced judgement and rejection for simply being us and this leaves a mark. Standing out, shining too bright, or being too much, doesn't feel safe and we're not sure it's worth the price.

When it comes to our dreams and the things we could do, we let the limiting beliefs and stories take over in our mind. Despite wanting more for ourselves and our life, we can't shake the fear of judgement, criticism, rejection and the worry of being alone. We're basing our life choices on what keeps us safe, not on what brings us joy.

These fears also arise when it comes to fully accepting ourselves too. We have so much to say and share and yet because this could cause conflict, or could be seen as controversial we decide that silence, or hiding is best. We loosen our boundaries and we begin to people please, each time losing another piece of ourselves. We're doing everything we can to simply fit in, blend in and have a safe comfortable life. At times life feels empty and again you ask the question *'Is this is'*? Without the confidence and conviction to speak up and just be you, you're living life by someone else's rules.

The fear of judgement, rejection and criticism can run very deep, the clue is in finding out exactly what it means for you and what the deeper fear is? For some it may be about being accepted, belonging and fitting in, for others it may be about avoiding conflict and arguments. Reflect on everything you've read so far in this book and captured in your journal, because already you'll already have noticed themes and reoccurring thoughts arising.

I know how uncomfortable it can be to explore old emotions and painful memories, but when you can let go of these, and identify what you're trying to protect yourself from, you'll reclaim your inner power. You'll suddenly become free to live life on your terms. It doesn't mean that you're no longer aware of judgement, rejection and criticism, it just means it no longer holds you captive.

We often think of freedom as being able to do what we want, when we want, but I believe it's much deeper than that. True freedom is about living every part of your life in a way that feels right for you and being able to be yourself while doing it. I don't know about you, but trying to be someone I wasn't for approval, love and security was exhausting. I was holding onto all this heavy energy in my body, because I was holding back and not speaking my truth. It felt like I was constantly coughing or trying to release a fur ball from my throat; energy has a funny way of making itself known and getting your attention.

Let me share the example of Caroline, she came to me with the belief that no one was truly listening to her. They were hearing her speak, but never listening. She felt ignored, overlooked, insignificant and she was so frustrated with everyone. When we dived into this a little more through our sessions, it became clear that Caroline was not listening to herself with some pretty big things in her life. She was ignoring her intuition and she rarely spoke her truth. She was so terrified of conflict and of hurting people's feelings that she metaphorically bit her tongue. Her whole upper body was tense and tight, she was constantly clenching her jaw and had even started to grind her teeth. This is another example of where the body is trying to get your attention. Part of Caroline was desperate to speak her truth, but staying safe won over every time. She was scared of judgement, rejection and what she feared was inevitable criticism.

Can you identify with Caroline in anyway? Perhaps you feel unheard and overlooked, or maybe, you're not listening to your own intuition and inner wisdom? Perhaps you also fear rocking the boat and having people disagree with you. My personal belief is that how you feel about yourself, is more important than other people's views and opinions. Ultimately you have to spend the rest of your life with you and you have to like the person staring back at you in the mirror.

Are you happy to go through the rest of your life being unseen and unheard by everyone around you? This is no way to live and to me this is not freedom, it's not even close. You've given away your right of self-expression and to speak your truth. You've imprisoned yourself and taken out your own tongue and who's to say that the views of others are right anyway.

There are so many examples I could share of where clients as young children have put themselves out there and consequently, they've been judged, humiliated and ridiculed. They felt rejected and because of this, they decided never to do anything like that again and certainly never to place themselves in such a position of vulnerability or visibility. This sort of thing happens all the time and to most people too, but as children we're simply not mature enough to be able to process what was really happening and it's harder to stay strong in the face of opposition and rejection. We make each nasty or snide comment mean that there must be something wrong with us. We're not acceptable, or enough.

Take Lara for example, as a child she was a free spirit, outspoken, determined and would dress however she saw fit. She loved to experiment with her look. After a humiliating experience with a teacher in front of her whole class, she made a decision that standing out was not safe, because it could lead to more humiliation and from that point on, she conformed. It's impacted her self-esteem, confidence and her ability to speak in public. It takes her right back to that earlier experience of being stared at, judged and with feeling that something was wrong with her.

I truly wish that more people had the self-awareness and emotional intelligence to fully appreciate the impact their words have on others. Often people speak without thinking and usually there are underlying stories, fears and beliefs going on for them. We'll look at this more closely in the next section.

Why other people choose to judge, criticise and reject others

I think it's useful to explore the things that may be going on psychologically for those who judge, reject and criticise others and perhaps why you've done this yourself in the past. Having a greater awareness here will help you deal with your fear and let you see that their response is not really about you, it will also make it easier to have compassion for people who are dealing with their own internal struggles. When you can see their reactions for what they truly are, your confidence will increase, you'll begin to trust yourself more and you'll understand how to deal with their behaviour and comments in a more empowering way.

Have you ever noticed that while some people in your life, love change and a bit of variety, there are others who create their entire life around routine, structure and certainty? Even if their life is making them unhappy, at least they know what to expect within every situation and circumstance, and with every person. When you start to change and grow, you begin to shake the very foundation of their life. Rather than look inwards at their own limitations and fears, they lash out at you because they want you to conform again and be the predictable person they have come to know. These people are not taking responsibility for how they feel and their emotions.

You might think this all sounds a little strange and you could be wondering how your choices and actions could trigger such an emotional response in others. Let's look at the underlying reasons in a bit more depth and bring things to life, you might then start to recognise people who this applies to:

- They're threatened by your growth and what it says about them. When you decide to face your fears and take action, you and your life begins to change. This can make some people very uncomfortable because it highlights to them where they're choosing not to take action in life. They're choosing the safe and predictable path and may instead be stuck in victim mode. With both of you making the same choices, there was a comfort in that for them. They could justify their own inaction, because you weren't taking action either. When they no longer have that excuse, they're presented with an opportunity to look inwards. The easy option is to lash out and criticise, hoping that you decide against taking action and so they too are let off the hook and can instead enjoy their safe and predictable life again. Most people are not malicious and would not consciously do this, they're just coming from a place of fear.

- They wonder if you'll still have space in your life for them. Watching someone else grow and change, can often make others worry if there will still be a space in your life for them. They imagine new friends and new experiences, which they may not get to be a part of. The criticism and judgement is usually a cry for reassurance.

- The rules have changed and they're not sure of themselves or the relationship anymore. As you become less worried about judgement, criticism and rejection, there's a very strong chance that your boundaries will also have shifted. There will be behaviours that you'll no longer accept from people and they may have to change how they treat you. Any change in boundaries is always confusing, because the other person is constantly trying to work out what is and is not acceptable now. They may feel on edge and also angry that the relationships dynamics have changed. Perhaps they knew that you would always be there to listen to them moan and complain, or perhaps you would do anything they asked. If these things change, they have to get their needs met elsewhere and there is uncertainty in this.

- They're worried about the decisions you're making and how those decisions impact them and their life. In these cases, their sense of safety is threatened, they're suddenly thrown into unknown waters and life has become unpredictable. Ultimately, they feel unsettled and unsure. For example, you're desperate to apply for a certain job, you know it would make you incredibly happy and that you would be amazing at it. On the one hand your partner is delighted for you and happy that more money could be coming into the household, but on the other hand they're worried and scared. This new job means they have to do more of the household chores and the childcare, it also means you'll be staying away from home one night a week. Suddenly their life and what they have become used to has shifted. They're feeling very uncertain, unsettled and perhaps having to deal with other emotions that weren't there before, such as; envy, jealousy or resentment. Their natural response is to try and stop whatever is causing these feelings and so they make comments that make you doubt your decision to apply for the job.

- They're scared for you. No one wants to see someone they care about fail or be upset. Some people are so worried by this, that they can wrap their loved ones up in cotton wool. What they're really saying is *'I don't know how I will cope if you fail or hurt yourself'*. Think about the parent who doesn't let their child go on the school trip, because they will miss them or will worry too much. The child was originally really excited to go away with friends, but now their mum has filled their head with worry and so the child decides to stay home.

- Not everyone looks at the world in the same way and certainly wouldn't make the same decisions. Sometimes they project their own views of life onto you and again their judgement and criticism is based on them. They wouldn't choose to make that decision, because if it was them, they would be overcome with fear. For example, the parents who judge and criticise their children for deciding to follow their passions in life instead of following a more traditional career path. They're fearful that their children will fail, won't have the nicer things in life and won't create security and stability for themselves. These are all projections.

- Reject before you're rejected. This is a classic defence mechanism. They're so worried that there's no longer a space in your life for them, that they decide to reject you before you reject them. In those moments it can be very hard because you'll want to take it personally. Remember, this is about where they're at and what is going on internally for them, it has no reflection on you. With some of those people it will be appropriate to reassure them and talk about their fears, with others it may be time to lovingly let them go from your life.

Can you begin to see how having a deeper understanding of what's going on for others, helps you to express and feel more compassion towards them? It literally diffuses the energy they're directing at you, because you can see it for what it really is. It can also stop you feeling so much fear about the choices you wish to make.

Exercise

Take some time now for some self-reflection and to answer these questions. As always capture your insights in your journal:

1. What worries you most about someone judging, rejecting or criticising you?
2. When was the first time you can remember feeling judged, rejected or criticised?
3. Who was there and what was it about?
4. How does your body respond when you think you are being judged, rejected or criticised?
5. Have you tried to protect yourself since then from the shame of judgement, rejection and criticism? How do you do this?
6. Are there certain people where these things bother you more? Does this surprise you?
7. Think about the people who do judge, reject or criticise you? Can you start to see where there may be more things at play? For example, your partner is worried about how your new job will affect them. Or your best friend is worried that if you take up a new hobby, you might make new friends and not have as much time for her?
8. If you believe there are more things at play, what could you do, to make this easier for both of you?
9. Does being seen or visible, make you feel exposed and vulnerable? If so, what fear sits underneath that?
10. Do you ever worry that people aren't really listening to you, or aren't interested in you? For many people, feeling unheard is a painful form of rejection.

> 11. How are all these fears stopping you from truly being you?

Remember, I'll share some practical tips and tools in the final part of this chapter. We're now going to explore another common fear, which is the fear of failure.

Fear of failure

The fear of failure can be crippling when we're trying to make those big decisions in life. Whether this is about choosing to leave a relationship, embarking on training for new skills, changing career, or even walking our true path and finally deciding to share our work, our gifts, and our purpose with the world. The fear of not succeeding and failing can keep us stuck and destined to a life of sitting on the side lines. We choose surviving over thriving, we choose mediocre instead of amazing, and we watch as everyone else goes out there and achieves success and lives the life we so desperately want.

It can feel totally crushing and yet we often have no one to blame but ourselves. We're the ones who chose to procrastinate, to let opportunities pass us by and to walk the safe path. We chose security, safety and comfort over change and taking action. Many other fears will play into this too, because people can get fixated on the fear of being seen, rejected, choosing the wrong path, feeling humiliated, disappointing others, or feeling guilt and shame.

Let's look at a couple of examples, before I share some questions with you. I want you thinking about what resonates for you, what triggers any kind of emotional response for you and what needs your attention:

- Many people associate failing with not being good enough. When failure strikes it doesn't matter what else is going on and what else could have impacted things, they've already decided that the failure was all about them. This brings up so many other feelings of not being worthy and of their dreams never becoming a reality.

- Some of my clients are so driven by being perfect that failure makes them feel incredible shame. For these people they will either procrastinate on taking action, or they over work and over give, taking them to a place of burnout and exhaustion. They are doing everything they can to avoid feelings of shame and humiliation that could come with failing. They fear that others are waiting to judge their failure and point the finger at them. The trouble with this is that whatever they do, it's never enough. They will always pick holes in their own achievements and believe they could have done more.

Both of these examples connect back to things we looked at in earlier chapters. While some people have an enormous amount of resilience and will find a way to bounce back, or to make things happen, there are others that take any failure to mean that their desires will never come to them. It's so final in their mind and so their choice to procrastinate keeps the dream alive. You can't fail and be deprived of your dream, if you've not yet taken steps to make it happen.

Exercise

Reflect on the following questions around failure and failing. Notice what you feel, what memories arise and capture your insights in your journal:

1. Why does it matter if you were to fail?
2. Where are you currently playing small and hiding away in the shadows? Are you doing this because it feels safer than people seeing you fail, or having to deal with the feeling of failure?

3. Is this really about the fear of failing, or are there other things you're trying to avoid feeling or dealing with?
4. Are you fighting against perfectionism? If so why? Reflect back to the section on perfectionism if you aren't sure.
5. Where have you felt this fear of failure before?
6. If you weren't afraid to fail, what action would you take today?

You should now have a better insight into your own fear of failure and what this brings up for you. I'm going to share some reframes that will encourage you and help you to move forward. We'll look at the practical tips at the end of this chapter:

- If you worry that you're not good enough, firstly ask yourself if this is a legitimate fear. If it is, then what can you do to make yourself good enough. For example, maybe you need to study or train more, perhaps you need to practice your skills, or get advice. If you can identify a gap, then do everything you can to bridge that gap. This will ensure that you feel confident moving forward. Add any insights to your journal and your action plan.

- True failure is not starting at all or giving up at the first hurdle. This doesn't mean that your dream won't happen, it just means it won't happen in the way, or in the time frame you had hoped for.

- Just know that failure is all part of creating success. We need to fail to know what does and doesn't work. I choose to see failure as a signpost to what I need to focus my attention on, or how I need to improve.

We're now moving onto our final fear in this chapter and it's one that most people struggle to understand, because it makes no logical sense to them. Let's dive in and see if any of this resonates for you.

Fear of being happy and having everything you've ever wanted

Some of you may be thinking that this fear is crazy, why would anyone block success, but actually this is much more common that you might think. People have an internal conflict going on, between wanting something and then pushing it away or blocking it. A more typical term for this is self-sabotage and we'll be coming onto that topic in the next chapter.

Part of the reason for blocking what they really want is all the uncertainty associated with change, not knowing what that new life would look and feel like, who they would have to become and a fear that it won't last anyway. When you commit to changing your life, you don't get all the answers in advance and you have to be willing to sit in uncertainty and this can feel uncomfortable for some people. You have to trust in the process and know that everything will turn out exactly as it's meant to. If being able to predict the outcome of things makes you feel safe, then changes in life, even if good, are going to be a challenge for you.

Believe me I do understand this fear, I have felt it many times myself and I see it all the time with clients. Thoughts such as, who will I be, what will others expect from me, who will no longer be in my life, or what sacrifices will I have to make. All of these thoughts can take over our mind and rather than enjoy the changes that are occurring, we're caught up in anxiety and fear. When this happens, we're not choosing happiness, in fact we're sacrificing it.

This whole book is based on choosing happiness and part of choosing happiness is choosing to face those challenging moments along the way, because you deeply desire what's on the other side of that. When you commit to becoming more self-aware, you know exactly what things or events are likely to test you and make you doubt yourself and so you can be prepared for this.

Exercise

Take some time to read through these questions and then to do the meditation that follows. These exercises will give you clarity over any fears you have about living your ideal future and why you may be resisting change. Answer the questions first, reflect and capture any insights in your journal. Then move onto the meditation.

Think back to chapter one and the exercise you did about your ideal day, bring those insights into your awareness, or refer back to your journal. Once you have a strong feel for this vision again, take a deep breath and then ask yourself the following questions:

1. Is there someone significant who is no longer in your life, how does this feel to you?
2. How does the future you feel, emotionally and physically?
3. When you think about a thriving business or career, with plenty of money coming in and being in demand, what comes up for you? Are you scared about what this could mean for your life, your relationship and your family?
4. What situations are no longer in your life?
5. Are you scared about the process of making these changes happen?
6. Are you scared that the dream won't last? That someone might take it away from you, or that you'll end up ruining it somehow?

Don't worry if the answers didn't come immediately, this meditation will help you to gain more clarity on any resistance:

1. Close your eyes and take some nice deep cleansing breaths. In through the nose and out through the mouth. Just feel your body relaxing.
2. Let go of the thoughts of the day and give yourself permission to be fully present and set the intention of being open to clarity.
3. Know that you're deeply grounded, imagine roots coming from the soles of your feet and connecting you to the earth if it helps. This is especially useful if you have a busy mind.
4. Know that you're safe, imagine a bubble of energy all around you keeping you safe and supporting you as you go through this process.
5. Bring into your mind's eye a vision of your dream life. Reflect on everything you already know you what and desire. Feel into that vision and notice the responses in your body. Walk through parts of that day or life if it helps. It's time to embody the future you.
6. Ask your intuition to show you where you're resisting due to your fear of success. You can use the questions above as a guide and notice where your mind turns to fear, or your body begins to contract.
7. Notice what you see in your mind's eye and what memories or people appear in your thoughts. Pay attention to any other feelings and emotions too, as these can also hold clues. These are all things that require some inner work and healing so that you can move on without this fear of success.

Fear of success can often feel emotionally painful because you know that you're the one in control with this and you're the one holding yourself back from the life you truly want. For those of you who are already very self-aware, I'm sure you have times where you know exactly what you're doing, and you just can't figure out why. You're likely to spend time and energy beating yourself up about your lack of action and then feeling even worse about yourself.

Overcoming fear

In this final section, we are going to look at a variety of ways that you can overcome fear. Not every example will be relevant to what you're dealing with and some suggestions will resonate more for you than others. The list gives you choice and you can always refer back to it:

- Trust yourself and your intuition. Self-doubt is a huge barrier to making decisions. Trusting yourself is about listening to your intuition and the messages that your body is communicating to you. Most of us experience gut feelings or hunches, so I invite you to pay more attention to these and to your body so that you can learn to trust yourself again. Intuition is like a muscle you need to work it. Here are some simple things that you can do to get started with this:

    o Notice how your intuition is communicating with you.
    o Follow your intuition with some of the smaller decisions in life. Just notice how things turn out. Remember intuition and trusting yourself is something that takes practice and time.

- Let go of the outcome. This is something that we'll explore in more depth later in the book, because it deserves a whole chapter of its own. For now, I'm only going to introduce the concept and get you thinking about what this means for you and how it would feel to do this. I'm sure you already know how easy it is to get attached to the outcome of your decisions. You want certain things to happen in a certain way, in a certain time. The trouble is, when reality doesn't meet your expectations, suffering happens. You feel angry, resentful and disappointed that things aren't going the way you wanted them to. This is when you need to let go of what you think has to happen and become open to something more coming to you. Sometimes life has a better plan, so make sure you're open enough to receive it.

- Know that when you're decisive and you make decisions, you give others the permission to be decisive too. I want you to think about the people that matter the most to you in life; your kids, your family, your friends, work colleagues, your clients, what kind of example do you want to set them? Would you like to teach them that they're powerful, that they're in control of their life and that they have the ability to choose and create a life which makes sense to them? What about giving them the inner resolve to know that if they choose and fail, this is okay too? If you want the people around you to feel this, the best gift you can give them is your own example. The world needs more people who are prepared to show others what is possible.

    o Reflect on all those decisions that you still haven't made because of fear. Write a list if it helps.
    o After starting to look at this section is there anything on that list where you feel ready to make a decision, because you now understand the fear behind it?

- If you can sense that significant people in your life are judging you due to their own fear, then thank those people for their concerns, but assert that this is something you really want to do and that you would appreciate their support. You can reassure them about the relationship, and if you know this decision affects them, you can reassure them that you will sit down and discuss the changes and any solutions needed.

- Surround yourself with positive uplifting people. Go to new events, clubs and gatherings and you'll find yourself drawn to people who are like minded. Choose to spend time with people who bring you joy, who encourage you to grow and expand and who love life.

- Know that it's okay and safe to assert your boundaries in a calm and loving way. This is not about getting aggressive or angry, it is about reinforcing what is and is not acceptable to you.

- If people choose to reject you, try not to take it personally. Accept that when you choose happiness, some people will no longer be a good fit for you, and they will drift from your life. This clears a space for you to meet more like-minded people. Be open to that and don't grieve for what was lost, it wasn't serving you anymore anyway.

- Get digging and identify the real fear, underneath it all. What are you really worried about?

- Release the belief that you won't be able to cope. Think of all the things you have dealt with in the past. I'm sure at times it wasn't easy, and you wondered if you would cope, but you did get through it. Taking time to reflect on this will help you to see and remember that you're powerful, capable and courageous.

- Be mindful of the language you use, both with others and within your own mind. Choose positive, empowering and uplifting words as much as you can. For example, I will, I can, I'm so capable, I can do anything etc. The words you use can either lift you up, giving you the courage to take action, or crush you in a single sentence.

- Look at the situations where you feel totally out of control and see if there are practical things that you could do that make you feel more in control, safe or comfortable. You may not be able to control people or events, but at the very least you can control your responses.

- Challenge yourself every day to do something that is outside of your comfort zone. Take one small step at a time, because with each step forward you create change and you grow. This could be as simple as changing your daily routine, changing the route you drive to certain places, picking a different parking spot, asking the new person at work if they want to have lunch together. Start small, gain your confidence and then keep pushing your boundaries.

- Use energy clearing modalities to help you release your fears. My favourites are things such as EFT/Tapping, Reiki, Meditation and Breath Work. The key, as I've said before is ensuring the modality resonates for you and the practitioner holds a safe space for you.

- Stop resisting change. You cannot stay alive and resist change. Even growing older is change. You have to start getting comfortable with being uncomfortable, uncertain and unsure. To help you with this, you need to figure out how to feel safe at your core. For me this is about ensuring my connection with source/the divine is strong and that I meditate regularly. When I don't do this for a few days in a row, I feel more anxiety, resistance to change and generally I lack trust and faith that all will be well.

- Have faith and trust in something bigger than you. If you knew that you were supported whatever decision you made, it would be much easier to get out there and take action. I also believe that everything happens for a reason. I don't always know what the reason is, but I choose to trust and have faith that one day I will look back and understand why things turned out the way they did. My faith in spirituality has helped me view life and the challenges I have come up against very differently. I have a sense of peace and acceptance around things that most people don't.

- Know that the choice is yours. Ultimately, there comes a point when you have to ask yourself what feels more painful, the fears within you, or the knowledge that you're not fulfilling your potential or purpose in life. Can you really live comfortably, knowing that you have within your grasp the chance to be and have so much more, but you're choosing to let fear dictate your life. Earlier in the book there was a meditation to help you capture your feelings if nothing was to change in your life. Use the emotions that came up within this to motivate you to take action and to face your fears around success.

- Ask for support and accountability. Without this it can be too easy to procrastinate and not take action. We slip back into old and bad habits and before we know it, another year has passed us by. Find someone who you know will give you the support and accountability you need.

With this comprehensive list of ways you can overcome fear, is there anything you would like to start doing differently immediately? Make a note of this in your journal, or even better declare your intentions to another, it's time to be the conscious creator of your own life and take back your inner power.

Chapter 5

Self-sabotage and upper limiting

"Self-sabotage is when we say we want something and then go about making sure it doesn't happen." Alyce P. Cornyn-Selby.

Put very simply, sabotage is where the conscious and subconscious mind are working in conflict with one another. For example, consciously we talk about wanting more money and wealth, but subconsciously we're actually doing things to ensure this never happens. Although we feel we're doing everything right, we're in fact setting ourselves up for failure. We just can't see it.

In this chapter we'll explore the concept of self-sabotage and upper limiting, more deeply, so that you'll feel confident in identifying these habits within yourself. We'll explore how these habits can and do relate to your mindset and your ability to choose happiness. I'll also show you how to spot sabotaging habits, explain why you might engage in these behaviour's and then look at how you can break the cycle. As with all areas of development, self-awareness here is absolutely key, because it means you can stop your habits before they gain any destructive momentum.

Self-sabotage is highly destructive and unfortunately very common. It's not enough to have a dream, you have to remove all the inner resistance that stands in the way between where you are, and where you want to be. Just think back to everything we've explored so far, being clear on who you are and what you want, having a positive mindset, overcoming limiting beliefs and facing your fears. If we don't master our thoughts, emotions and feelings, we can easily sabotage our self and not even notice.

Having the life you really want, is more than just taking focused action. It's about knowing with every fibre of your body that you deserve it and that it will happen for you. There can be no doubt if you are to have everything you dream of. You have to have the strength and resilience to move past every limiting belief, story and fear within you to ensure you never lose sight of where you want to be and to ensure that whatever happens you trust that the dream is still possible. Even when your current reality suggests that nothing is changing, you need to believe that things are coming together and will reveal themselves when the time is right.

Sabotage can be a really sneaky thing because often our personal flavour of sabotage, is hidden in our blind spots. Either we chose not to see what is right in front of us, or the behaviour and beliefs are so deeply ingrained, we just can't see it. There can also be a great deal of emotional avoidance taking place, because for many people, actually facing their pain feels too scary and intense. It can bring up feelings and beliefs that they aren't worthy or deserving enough. Which at their core makes them question if they are lovable and deserving of love. Sabotaging behaviours such as these, are driven by the subconscious, because it's trying to maintain normality and the emotional status quo.

As I've just mentioned, self-sabotage is a very hard thing to spot in ourselves and often when other people suggest that this is what we might be doing, we don't always receive this insight very well. We're likely to argue strongly against this, defending our actions and choices. We could even think the other person was looking for a fight, or wasn't being supportive. Our conscious mind would search for all the reasons that the other person doesn't know what they're talking about, because they don't have all the facts and they aren't living our life. In those moments we can lash out, because to accept the truth means we have to look within at why we're engaging in certain behaviours.

When I work with clients, I always ask permission to play devil's advocate and offer another viewpoint. I am always careful to choose my words wisely, especially with those that don't like being told what to do, or who only feel emotionally safe when they're in control. For example, I might say *'Is it possible,'* or, *'I'm wondering if'*, I'm giving them the space to see things clearly for themselves. When we feel empowered and as if we've uncovered the inner truth ourselves, we're more likely to make the necessary changes.

Being on the outside of things gives you an advantage. You aren't as emotionally attached to the situation and the choices being made and you aren't feeling the fear, or being impacted by the limiting beliefs. You can see the habits and behaviours for what they really are, sabotage and resistance in moving forward. As someone in the middle of things, we can often be in a place of denial. We've been living with our fears and limiting beliefs for so long, that they've become our truth and our prison. It's why this work is so important to me. I want to help you lift the veil and see the truth of who you are and what I already know is possible for you.

Our mind has two main power centres, the conscious mind and the subconscious mind and 95% of our decision-making power comes from the subconscious mind. The subconscious mind is all the beliefs, values and experiences that have made us who we are today. It's a very clever and a highly evolved piece of equipment and it will do everything it can to keep us safe, to avoid conflict and to prevent change. Even when change is necessary the subconscious mind will try and convince us that we should think twice before implementing anything. This is where I often see so much unfulfilled potential, because the subconscious mind has led people down a path of doubt and worry.

For many people you can get to the point where your subconscious has such a strong hold over you and you believe everything that your mind is telling you. The excuses you utter feel so real and genuine. It's in these moments that we need to have people around us who we trust and respect, so that when they call us out on our own excuses and stories, we pay attention and we listen. It might cause us some serious discomfort and it's likely that we'll lash out and get annoyed, but we need these people and their honesty. I can tell you from personal experience that being self-aware is not enough. We will only ever see what we want to see based on our inner programming and life experiences.

Without having support in your life to overcome this habit, you risk staying stuck forever. You should even be mindful of the self-sabotage that could stop you from completing this book and doing the suggested exercises. It's a well known fact that most people rarely finish a book that they start, some never even begin reading it at all. At the time of making the purchase they believed that the book could help them solve their problem. What they hadn't fully considered was that they would be the ones who had to do the work. Reading the words alone is not enough for deep and lasting change to take place.

You brought this book for a reason, so please commit to yourself and doing the inner work. It may not always feel fun or exciting to work through your emotions, feelings, thoughts and habits, but it's essential if you want to turn things around and have the life you want. Everything is always your choice, so what do you choose?

When you chose to commit to self-awareness and you own your own self sabotaging behaviour's, you suddenly regain control over the direction of your life and what's possible for you. You have become the deliberate creator of your own life and the power is back in your hands. You're no longer drifting through life at the mercy of your mind.

Before we go any further with self-sabotage, I want to share a little about upper limiting as this will give more explanation and context to what's happening for you emotionally when you sabotage.

Gay Hendricks, the author of The Big Leap, defines an upper limit problem (ULP) as the amount of success, happiness, money etc. that we will allow ourselves to experience before we sabotage things and bring ourselves back down, to a more comfortable, familiar and predictable level. Usually this amount is set in childhood and it sets the bar for what we will give ourselves permission to be, do and have later in life. When life gets too good, all our internal alarm bells start going off, telling us that we don't deserve more, we aren't worthy of more and that more is scary.

It's scary, because our mind has gone to a place of fear. Maybe we'll end up abandoned and alone by those who are meant to love us unconditionally, or we'll be judged, criticised or rejected for taking this path, or making this choice. To the subconscious mind, this all feels like disaster and threatens our inner desire for survival. Our sub conscious mind can be very dramatic and always goes to worst case scenario, because this is when it gets our attention.

As mentioned above, upper limiting rears its ugly head when life gets too good and this is usually when we're going through periods of growth, to be, do and have more than we're used to. Unfortunately, it's not a one-time thing either. If you're committed to yourself and growth, then every big period of change can and usually does, bring upper limiting. Let me share some example of life getting too good:

- You suddenly experience flow and ease when it comes to money. You have more than you need. There is money in the bank, and you have the ability to buy some of those things on your wish list.

- Your career and work are doing really well. You get the promotion or pay rise; your projects are going well, and you're finally getting the recognition and praise you desire.

- If you have your own business, it could be that you're selling out your programs, courses and services with ease. You have a wait list of clients and you're seen as the expert in your field.

- You finally have the perfect work life balance and you're no longer sacrificing health, relationships or your social life in order to get things done or earn more money.

- You're doing work that you love and feel passionate about. It feels like you're being paid to have fun.

- You feel happier and more content than you ever have. Life is flowing and you're truly in alignment with yourself and your values.

- You're having so much fun and life is full of laughter.

- You have the health and vitality you've always dreamed of. You're prioritising self-care and feeling the benefits.

- Your relationship is going well, and you feel deeply loved. You have incredible chemistry with your partner and a genuine connection that feeds your soul.

- You have such amazing and supportive people in your social circle. They fully support and accept you.

- New opportunities are presenting themselves in every direction and these are taking your life to exciting new heights.

It's in these moments that a quiet voice inside of us starts to speak and once again we focus on our ingrained belief that we can't have it all, that we aren't worthy or deserving and that something has to give. If we have not done enough inner work and aren't self-aware, then the old fears and beliefs can take hold. This is when we begin to look for external evidence to confirm our fears and beliefs.

We self-sabotage, because survival, feeling safe and being in a familiar place in our life, is our number one priority. Just remember your subconscious mind hates change and the more work you do on yourself to create growth, the more it will try and tear you down. It will try and make you think that you aren't strong enough to create change or stick to change. The subconscious mind wants its basic needs met. It wants to know that it has somewhere safe and warm to live, that there is always hot water for showers, clean water for drinking and enough food to eat. When we're living from a place of getting our basic needs met, there is no space for our dreams and a bigger vision, it's all about survival. We try and kid ourselves that living this way is acceptable and that we should be thankful for what we have, but inside we're dying a little more each day.

I truly believe that our soul wants to live and experience the fullness of life, because we all have a purpose and a contribution to make. When we give into sabotage, we're betraying ourselves, our potential and we're denying the world of our uniqueness. I want you to live a life that brings you immense joy, where you feel alive and connected to yourself. I want you to make all your decisions from a place of love and not from fear and I want you to know that you're making a difference to others. Let me share what these behaviour's look like, so you can identify them for yourself.

What does self-sabotage and upper limiting look like?

My aim for the next few sections, is that you will increase your own self-awareness around self-sabotaging and be able to spot things before they get out of hand. There is something very powerful about being able to clearly see what you're doing and then choose a different response.

The examples below are things I see my clients and people around me deal with all the time. The reasons behind the act can be very different, because we all have very unique psychological needs that we're trying to meet, but how it looks is very similar. Many of these things we've already covered in previous chapters, but it's good to address them again, so that you can see how destructive these things are and it gives you an opportunity to ensure you've dug deep enough with those earlier topics.

While there are many types of self-sabotage, one of the most common is procrastinating and so it seems only fitting that we start there.

Procrastinating

The general definition of procrastination is, the action of delaying or postponing something. Taking this one stage further, I believe the action of delaying or postponing can be applied to starting something, or even stopping something, so let me explain more.

One aspect of procrastination is choosing not to start taking action on something that you know you should be doing, or that could be beneficial or good for you. For example, you need to finish that project at work, finally make a decision which has occupied your thoughts for weeks, look at your finances and create a plan, put more effort into your relationship, or start an effective self-care program. All of these things would enrich and improve your life if you committed to them.

The other side of procrastination is about choosing not to stop doing something that you know you should. For example, wasting time scrolling through social media and being on the internet, spending time with or working with toxic and demanding people, wasting money on things you don't need and eating far too much junk food. Stopping these things, would again bring great benefits to your life.

With both of these scenarios, you constantly put off starting or stopping something and come up with a variety of excuses or reasons as to why you can't or shouldn't take action. Instead you're choosing to stay within your comfort zones. I have no doubt that life feels very safe, but the trouble is you're choosing to sacrifice growth, expansion and those exciting rewards that come with it. Without committing to taking action, to ourselves and to our dreams of more, we risk waking up to the same life every day. We will continue to feel stuck, lost and empty, because we're struggling, or refusing, to connect with the full meaning of our existence. Instead we're choosing survival and safety.

The things that you know you should be starting or stopping, are your energy drains or leaks. They literally drain you of energy as you constantly think about them and what you should do. It also takes energy to keep coming up with excuses, especially ones that you can believe yourself. These things constantly nag at you and you're always trying to defend your choices, mostly in your own mind.

I'm sure this has started you thinking about some of the things you're procrastinating on. Keep those in mind because we'll explore these more shortly. To ensure you have a clear understanding of procrastination and feel confident to spot this behaviour in yourself, let me share some examples. These tend to be the excuses I've heard the most from others, but also things I find myself saying and feeling:

- I'm too tired
- I don't have the energy for it
- I don't know where to start
- I feel overwhelmed
- I don't have time
- I can't do it
- I don't feel like it
- Now's not the right time for me

- There are too many other things going on right now
- I don't have clarity and so I don't want to make a bad decision or go off down the wrong path
- I can't think clearly or focus
- I just need to do some more mindset work or inner healing first
- I need to complete this task first, then I can do that
- I'm sacred of making the wrong decision

The crazy thing here is that by getting the task done or even taking baby steps towards your goal, you potentially achieve success, more money and happiness, the very things you say you want. Plus, you wouldn't have to deal with all the guilt and shame you place on yourself, for not taking any action and for actually buying into the excuses you tell yourself. The indecision of whether to do something or not is exhausting, so as the NIKE slogan says *'Just Do It'*.

It's ironic that every day I help people with self-sabotage and procrastination, and yet this book has taken me far longer that it should have to complete. So, when I say I understand your internal struggles, I really do. I used pretty much every excuse on that procrastination list above, as to why I couldn't just sit down and get it written. I knew consciously what I was doing, and boy was I getting annoyed with myself, but ultimately, I was afraid. I was afraid that this book wouldn't help people, that I would waste hours writing something that no one would read and the biggest fear of all, I might just actually become successful and then be able to devote more time to writing and have the aligned business I really desired.

With all the change and uncertainty that the world experienced in 2020, people needed emotional support and healing more than ever. They needed tools to help them choose happiness and to know how to reconnect with their inner truth. Despite knowing that my book would help and was needed, I still procrastinated. You can see from my own example, that there are always underlying reasons for our choices. The key as I've already shared is self-awareness, a commitment to your purpose in life and accountability. I am so grateful for the people in my life who hold me accountable and give me a loving kick when I get in my own way.

Exercise

Now that you have a clear understanding of what procrastination is and how this can play out in your own life, let's go a little deeper for you. In your journal, list all the areas of your life, such as work/career, relationships, health, friendships, hobbies and social life, self-care, boundaries, inner healing etc. Now take some time to answer the following questions.

Remember, the more time you give this and the deeper you delve, the more you'll uncover about yourself. Self-knowledge is power. The behaviour you're displaying in one area of your life, is very likely to be seeping into other areas too:

1. Where are you procrastinating in your own life? Reflect on the things you're not starting and the things you're not stopping.
2. Reflect on how procrastination is impacting you and limiting you? What are you not being, doing or having because of this?
3. What impact is your procrastination having on those closest to you?

Writing this down and seeing it in black and white can often give you the wake-up call you need. Now that you've started to gain some clarity on where you're holding yourself back through procrastination, we're going to explore seven other ways that you sabotage and upper limit. We'll then begin looking at why you engage in these behaviour's and what's really going on within you. Some of these seven areas can be harder to spot, accept or admit to than others, so just approach all of this with a curious and open mind.

While exploring these seven areas of sabotage and upper limiting, you might realise that this is how or why you procrastinate too. Everything that we're looking at in this chapter is linked and overlaps, so just make a note of it in your journal and I promise everything will come together and become clear. At the end of each section, just take a moment before reading on, to really be honest with yourself about whether you engage in that behaviour.

Blaming

We all know people who are experts at the blame game and we've probably done this a few times ourselves too. It's essentially the inability to take responsibility for their choices and actions, or lack thereof, and so they blame people and situations outside of themselves. The following are some of the most common things I hear and have used:

- My children are demanding all my time and attention.
- My husband or partner is not supporting me enough.
- The economy is failing and there isn't enough disposable money available for people to buy from me. At the time of doing the final edits for this book it was 2020 and the UK was in partial lock down to aid with slowing the spread of the virus. The lack of disposable money was a huge fear and belief for those with businesses. There was of course some reality to this, but it was also a time when I saw some people and businesses thrive and make more money than ever.
- My competitors are taking all the available business and I can't compete.
- My boss doesn't value or appreciate me. I feel completely overlooked.

- I have a total lack of clarity, focus and motivation. I just feel like I'm wading through treacle and waiting for inspiration to hit.
- I don't have enough money and I can't invest in the help and support I need.

While I totally appreciate that some life transitions and events will of course impact your focus and motivation to take action, you also need to be honest with yourself in terms of how much you're letting it impact you and for how long. We should always acknowledge our emotions and how we feel, but it's essential we don't get lost in our emotions. Once we've processed and begun healing, we need to move on with life again. The time needed for this will of course vary and it's why a deep connection with yourself is essential. You can then be honest about whether more healing time is required, or whether sabotage has taken hold and you've slipped into blame.

Numbing out and avoiding our emotions

When we choose to numb our emotions, what we're really choosing to do is ignore how we feel. We're suppressing our feelings and we've decided that the safer option is avoidance. To the outside world we look like we're okay and that we're coping with life, but actually we feel empty and lost. The process of numbing means that we don't have to experience the emotions that cause us the most pain, but the sacrifice is the inability to experience the emotions that fill our hearts with love and joy. It's a huge price to pay, but feeling safe and in control, often takes priority.

People will often choose this option, when the intensity of their emotions feels too big to handle. They're scared of what they feel now and where this could take them. They fear they won't be able to cope with the emotional pain and hurt, because they've been bottling it up for years. For some it could also be a lifelong habit to deny their emotions and to pretend all is well, just think about those with a low self-esteem and who don't want to be a burden to others.

Some people will also be placing judgement on their emotions. For example, they may have an underlying belief that it's not safe, or acceptable to feel anger or rage. Instead they have chosen to swallow down their emotions and internalise things instead. As a sensitive soul I can easily sense and feel blocked anger within another person. Their body language, facial expressions, tone of voice and entire way of being gives them away every time, but often they will deny this inner anger. Some people don't want to admit that they feel angry and others are completed disconnected from what they feel. In both cases they expend a vast amount of energy denying it, but their energy and their body never lies. I have a huge belief in the mind body connection and suppressed emotions always have a way of making themselves known eventually. You just have to know what to look for.

When we choose to numb how we feel, we're also avoiding making changes or moving forward with life. Without feeling things such as desire, focus, determination or even things like boredom, anger and injustice, we're avoiding change. We don't have enough drive to take risks and make more conscious choices for our self. It's a classic form of sabotage and procrastination.

There are a number of ways we can choose to numb out:

- Deny our emotions completely.

- Project how we feel onto other people. I have seen other people claim that the other person is the one who is sad, angry, negative or in a place of fear, when in fact they're seeing their own emotions being mirrored back to them in that other person.

- Get really busy, by over working and over giving so that there is no time left for self-exploration and honesty.

- Overeating, or eat foods that we know aren't good for us, so that we change our physiology and instead focus on the feeling of being full, sick or in discomfort or pain.

- Engaging in any another addiction, which distracts us from our emotions and thoughts.

Fighting addictions

First of all, I want to be clear that I am not an addictions expert and we are only touching on this subject lightly to highlight where you're sabotaging and hitting an upper limit. If you know you're struggling with addiction and it's seriously impacting your mental and physical well-being, then please seek out the help of a licensed professional.

Often we think of addictions as being drugs, smoking or alcohol, but the reality is, we can become addicted to anything. The aim is always to avoid addressing how we really feel. We're using the addictions as a way to escape life and to change our emotional, spiritual and mental state. For some people they're using the addiction as a replacement for what they truly crave. For example, love, joy, respect, connection, pleasure, fun, excitement etc. Or even comfort, security or reassurance. By engaging in the addiction, a need has been met and so this becomes the fix that they seek. For others they can be using their addictions as a way to avoid their feelings, as we've already discussed in the previous section.

People can be reluctant to release their addictions, because they just don't believe there is another way to achieve the same emotional, physical or spiritual state. They may have the self-awareness that life has to change, and this requires action, but they're scared of giving something up that means they'll finally have to take a good long look at themselves and their life. This makes them feel very uncertain, out of control and scared. It can feel much easier to stay stuck within the addiction cycle, because as least that's predictable and familiar.

These are some of the most common addictions I see on a daily basis. Just notice if any of these resonate for you:

- Drugs
- Alcohol
- Cigarettes and vaping
- Caffeine
- Sugar
- Junk food
- Scrolling endlessly on social media
- Binge watching Netflix
- Being busy for the sake of being busy
- Over working
- Needing adrenaline, stress, or pressure to get things done
- Engaging in dangerous activities, purely to feel more alive and to get that buzz
- Sexual gratification and porn

Attracting or creating drama, stress or conflict into your life

It felt like life had turned a corner and you were finally happy. Everything was flowing with ease and there was stillness and peace in your life. It was almost too good to be true and if you're honest with yourself, part of you was waiting for something to go wrong.

This peaceful and happy life was an unfamiliar feeling for you, life just got too good and so your subconscious mind decided to reset things to a level that felt more comfortable and normal for you. Think back to what I shared about hitting an upper limit of what we will allow ourselves to experience. The easiest way to pull us away from a happy and peaceful life, is to create drama, stress and conflict. This can mean different things to different people, but ultimately, we're looking to create a negative situation, so that we can feel justified in feeling those heavy and dense emotions again; agitated, angry, anxious etc. Or we want life to return to what feels normal for us, even if that is a negative and toxic situation to most others.

This is more common than you might think, so read through the following examples and see if any resonate for you. Make a note in your journal if they do:

- You start an argument or heated discussion with another. Often, you already know how this is going to play out with the other person, which is exactly why you decided to do this. Part of you knew that the other person was always going to refuse you, disagree with you, or engage in the conflict. This is most often done with those closest to you, because they're easy and available targets, although I also see a great deal of this taking place on social media too.

- You can choose to stay in toxic relationships and friendships. You know that certain people aren't good for you and yet you stay connected with these people, emotionally, physically and energetically. They may be people who don't support you and are emotionally abusive, all of which makes you doubt yourself and impacts your confidence. These people are also very negative and tend to be energy vampires. You feel exhausted when you're with them, because they drain you of your life energy. Being with these people is not only familiar, it also holds you back, because you simply don't have the energy to fulfil your potential. A perfect way to sabotage and stop yourself from growth and change.

- You can place obstacles and challenges in your path that either don't need to be there, or you make mountains out of mole hills. Normally this is about making the obstacles bigger and more complicated than they need to be. If there are obstacles to deal with along the way, then this can stop you from doing the things that really matter. For example, knowing you need to do tackle some paperwork or your finances, but instead you decide that now is the perfect time to clean the house, sort the garden, or wash the car. These are small examples and seem valid enough, but if you're prone to this type of distraction and form of sabotage, you'll be amazed how big the obstacles can get.

- You might choose to play the victim and feel as if nothing is shifting or changing in your life. By taking on the role of victim, you choose to be powerless over being powerful. You've decided that solutions work for other people, but not for you and because of that there's no point in taking action, making big decisions, or taking any risks. You're actively getting in your own way and finding an obstacle for every solution. If you still feel like this habit is present for you, then refer back to the earlier section on playing the victim.

- You may become ill, or experience accidents. This is often your body's way of slowing you down and preventing you from doing more. It's also a way that it keeps you physically safe and from pushing your body too hard. You might experience health conditions such as IBS, adrenal fatigue and other such autoimmune disorders. Your body is in fight or flight and attacking itself.

- Unexpected expenses keep cropping up. You thought you were going have a surplus of money, or enough to pay the bills without struggle, but before you know it, an unexpected expense comes up. This takes you back to a place of struggle again, which is a very familiar feeling.

- Having a general feeling of discomfort, worry and anxiety. You started to feel too good, too content and this is simply a feeling that you're not used to. The mind searches for something it can worry or fret about to bring you back down to what feels normal for you.

Playing down your abilities and gifts

When you start playing down your abilities to others and yourself, you don't have to step into that next version of you. You've convinced yourself and others that you don't have what it takes to live a different life. You get to feel safe within the life that you've created, but at the same time, you'll be pushing away potential opportunities for growth, expansion and for greater health, wealth and happiness.

This can feel soul crushing at times, because while you try and deny your abilities, you know you have more to offer. Limiting beliefs, lack of confidence, fear and now sabotage has taken over. Let's recap on some key areas that cause you to self-sabotage when it comes to your abilities and gifts. Make a note of any insights in your journal:

- Engaging in negative self-talk. You tell yourself that you can't do something or shouldn't do something. By listening to that inner critic, you're playing into the hands of self-sabotage. Your conscious mind actually starts to believe that you're not smart enough, clever enough, or good enough and so it keeps you trapped. Reflect back to the chapter on limiting beliefs and see if there is more self-exploration and releasing that needs to be done. As we grow and expand there will always be more to heal and release, because we're choosing to live a bigger life.

- Taking action with safe tasks. This is a fascinating thing to observe, because often people will claim they're taking action and in truth they are. However, they're not taking action with the things that really matter. They're convincing themselves that smaller tasks need to be done first, or that they have equal priority. The reality is they're avoiding taking action with the things that really matter. For example, if you were looking to start dating again and were focusing on safe tasks, you might focus on getting your hair cut, buying new clothes, or working on your confidence. However, you never actually go on dates, join dating sites, or place yourself in a position to meet a new partner. This is something I see a lot within the online business space too, take Chloe for example. She spent so much time tweaking her website, creating marketing strategies, planning for the future and doing other administrative tasks. All of which helped her to run a smooth business, but it did not get the new clients into her community, or onto her mailing list. She needed to be more present on social media, doing interviews, podcasts, creating videos, creating content that shared who she was and her opinions. Being so exposed and visible terrified her, so she kept herself busy with safe tasks.

- Hiding away in the shadows as others live your dream life. You know that the key to being more successful is actually showing up and being more present in your own life and business, but instead you're hiding away in the shadows. You're not grasping the opportunities that are available to you and now you're feeling frustrated and envious as other people live your dream life. You probably find yourself getting triggered by the success of others and wanting to downplay their abilities, simply because it's easier to do this than admit you're the one not taking action and facing your fears.

Giving up

This is one of the things that I find the hardest to witness, because they're so close to the finish line and yet at the last minute people give up. They truly start to believe all the stories in their mind about why it isn't possible, or it won't happen and so they abandon their dream and goal. The fear took over and it won.

When I see this happening in people, I know that while limiting beliefs and fears are undoubtably coming up, there's also a lack of commitment to the end result. We often hear people talking about their why, and this is exactly what's coming into play here. Every great and meaningful change, success and achievement came after failure, disappointments and setbacks. The question you need to ask yourself, is how much do you really want the end result? Is it a nice to have, or are you committed to making it happen no matter what?

If you want to know what this looks like, let me share some examples:

- You embark on an exercise and healthy eating regime and just before you reach your goal, you decide it's too hard and the end goal won't happen and so you quit. Before you know it, you're back to eating junk food and giving excuses to yourself about why you can't work out.

- You're so close to finishing a project and there are just the final pieces to work on, but before you have a chance to see it through, your mind gets in the way. You convince yourself that you can't do it, others won't like it, it won't work, and you should never have wasted your time.

- You've made a decision to make a big change in your life and you've put the wheels in motion, but at the last minute you get scared about all the changes that are heading your way. You wonder if you can cope, you start to feel overwhelmed and instead of committing to change and your new life, you pull the plug on everything. I've even seen people achieving the success they longed for and then sabotage themselves by going back to their old way of being when their negative thinking took over.

- You're learning a new skill, or trying to incorporate a new mindset and suddenly it all feels too hard and like it requires too much effort and so you give up. You choose to go back to your comfort zone and tell yourself that you didn't want to do this anyway, people won't want it, or you simply can't learn anything new.

Blocking receiving

This topic is vital when it comes to creating change and choosing to be happy, so we'll go deeper with this in another chapter. For now, I just want you to start thinking about where this could be happening for you.

When we don't allow ourselves to receive more in life, we're consciously and subconsciously holding ourselves back. We can often have everything we've ever wanted and asked for, right on our doorstep, but we're refusing to allow it into our life. To receive more means you have to deal with all your fears, doubts, guilt, and feelings of being worthy and deserving.

If you keep on listening to that voice in your head, making excuses and putting up barriers, you'll always feel like you're almost there, or always on the edge of something. This is an incredibly frustrating feeling. To almost be able to reach out and touch it, yet still have it out of reach.

Start reflecting on the following:

1. Do I allow myself to receive compliments from others?
2. Do I allow people to help and support me?
3. Do I grasp opportunities with both hands when they are presented to me?

Exercise

We've now looked at seven additional ways that you could sabotage and upper limit yourself and your life. If you haven't already, take some time to reflect on what these seven areas have brought into your awareness and answer the following questions. Capturing your insights in your journal:

1. In which areas of your life are you currently sabotaging, or struggling to move past your current upper limit?
2. What are your own personal traits and habits when it comes to self-sabotage?
3. Can you identify which of these are the most destructive and prevent you from feeling happy?
4. Can you see where your self-sabotaging is impacting other people?

Once you've taken the time you need and completed this exercise, read on and we'll look at why you engage in these sabotaging behaviours.

Why you sabotage and struggle to move past your upper limit

Looking at all the examples of self-sabotage and upper limiting, I think we can all agree that they're destructive behaviours to indulge in and yet often we still can't break the cycle. Don't forget that the behaviours you're choosing are about keeping you safe, and often there are psychological things going on beneath the surface, that impact your thinking and choices.

Even those with a high level of self-awareness can indulge in these behaviours without realising, none of us are immune to this. Understanding what we're trying to achieve by doing these things is vital in taking back control and stopping the sabotage. Have your journal at the ready and let's take a closer look at what is going on beneath the surface and within our subconscious mind. Don't be surprised if some of these underlying reasons for sabotage have already made themselves known in earlier chapters. This is to be expected and it gives you a more complete picture and understanding of yourself. Plus it ensures you haven't overlooked anything:

- I don't believe I deserve it. This connects in with low self-esteem and so when life suddenly looks and feels too good for us, we begin to self-sabotage to take it back down to a level that feels comfortable and acceptable. The belief of not deserving something, can be something that you've struggled with for years, or it could come after a run of bad luck. For example, the person who is made redundant and then tries to get another job, but repeatedly fails to get interviews. Their self-esteem takes a hit and when they're finally close to getting a job that makes them happy, they sabotage the interview, because they have come to believe they don't deserve it.

- You feel guilty at having so much in your lives, especially when you see those around you who are struggling. You wonder what makes you so special that you don't have to worry about money. Often this causes you to find drama and challenges in other areas of our life, so you don't stand out, so people don't judge you and so you feel better about being happy, successful or having money flow in with ease.

- You're battling with limiting beliefs. If your predominant thoughts are negative and are limiting, you'll allow yourself to believe the negative thoughts, such as; *'I am too old'*, *'I am not clever enough'*, *'I can't earn money that easily'*, and *'good things don't happen to people like me'*. The feelings that these beliefs create are so strong that you often feel too overwhelmed to break away from them and you can't even establish which ones are true anymore.

- You're overcome with fear. You're so scared by what the future could look like, that you completely give in to the stories you tell ourselves. We all have basic human needs that we're always trying to meet, such as feeling safe and secure. Taking positive action can take you away from our comfortable, familiar and predictable lives. You choose familiarity over change and risk. For many people, there can be a great deal of fear in actually having everything you desire, because you have no idea what the future would look like. You're scared and so you procrastinate and keep success and abundance at arm's length. We've already explored fear in the previous chapter, and this is a big reason for sabotaging. The subconscious mind takes over and convinces us that we have something to worry about and so we choose inaction. If necessary, go back through the chapter on fear and see which of those still resonate for you and use the information provided to work through your fears. Remember, your subconscious mind is trying to protect you and keep you safe. It wants you to believe the fears so that life never moves forward. Staying safe and surviving is your key priority, and this is further reinforced if you have responsibility for other people, as your decisions impact them too.

- You fear out-shining others. When you embrace the fullness of who you are, it can mean that other people get triggered. You don't want them to feel bad about themselves, because of your choices, or just for being you. Think about the sibling who is constantly being asked why they can't be more like you. You're also scared to leave people behind and be alone. Part of our human nature is to fit in and belong. When we grow and expand, there's a good chance that we won't have as much in common with our old friends anymore. Simply because we're not the same person anymore. We're scared to let go of friends, because there is a comfort in them, even if the relationship has become toxic.

- There are benefits of staying stuck. When I ask people, what are the benefits of staying stuck, they look at me like I've grown horns. They reply that there are no benefits to being overweight, for not earning the money they want and there are certainly no benefits of being in a relationship that is toxic and dysfunctional. The truth however, is that there are plenty of benefits if you know what you're looking for. Let me give you an example, the person who remains overweight because they can't stick to a diet and never gets to the gym. Some of the more obvious benefits of remaining overweight, are being able to eat whatever you want, and you don't have to go and sweat it out in the gym. The less obvious benefits are; you're avoiding being judged by others in the gym because you're so overweight, you're using food as a replacement for the love, intimacy and connection you crave and, you're terrified if you lose weight and your partner still has affairs then it must mean that at your core, you're not enough.

- You're driven by perfectionism. You're so scared of failing and everything not being perfect, that you decide it's less emotionally painful to keep everything the same and live with that stuck feeling. At least you won't have to beat yourself up for being a failure.

- You can remain in control. Knowing what to expect from life is very reassuring, even when it's no longer good for you. When you value safety and security above everything else, you'll always choose the path that is well trodden. There is a false sense of being in control and that life won't be able to throw you any nasty surprises. If you embrace the fullness of your potential, you'll have no idea who you'll become, or what expectations will be placed on you and this is scary.

- Secretly you like the drama and excitement. We all know people in our life who are always dealing with a drama and you get the sense that secretly they quite like it. In those moments they're choosing to value the energy of the drama over moving forward positively in their life. They'll strongly deny this, mainly because they don't even recognise they're doing it, but the drama is a short term way of meeting their needs for a bit of variety, adventure and excitement in their life. Could this be you too?

- You've reached somethings called your happiness set point. Which is the upper limit for what you'll allow yourself to experience. Although certain events can obviously cause you to feel very happy, or very sad, you'll always return to a familiar set point. For example, if happiness was a scale between one and ten, and your set point is five, then no matter what great things happen for you, for example, you get the amazing job and pay increase, you would find ways, consciously and subconsciously, to bring life back down to a five out of ten overall. Think about the person who has a great career, but awful marriage, or the person who has an amazing marriage and great friends, but is really struggling with their health. There always seems to be one area where they struggle.

Exercise

We've gone through lots of information in this chapter and I'm sure it's given you much to think about. Having this information and an increased level of self-awareness, will give you all the tools you need to change your future and to choose happiness. It's time to complete our final exercise around sabotaging and upper limiting, so let's look at the following questions to gain a better understanding of what thinking is taking place in your subconscious mind:

1. Reflecting on all the ways that you currently sabotage yourself; can you identify what your inner thinking is, or why you're sabotaging? Use the list above if it helps.
2. Just for fun, can you spot others in your life who are self-sabotaging? Being able to identify these people, allows you to express more compassion for them, especially when you begin to consider their motivation for sabotaging.

A word of warning though. To finally start seeing where you're self-sabotaging in your own life can be hugely empowering. You may feel so excited with this newfound knowledge and feel compelled to start offering your wisdom to others, especially when you can clearly see that they're self-sabotaging. Just be warned, they're unlikely to be receptive to your wisdom and you may find yourself in the middle of quite a bit of conflict. Remember gaining permission to offer an alternative view is essential and some people just aren't ready to do the inner work. All you can do is accept them, love them unconditionally and be there if they need you.

How to move past self-sabotage and overcome your upper limits

Now that you've explore where you might have been blocking yourself, I want to share some simple things you can do now, to move past this destructive behaviour and become a more deliberate creator of your own life. As I've mentioned before, some of these ideas and tips are repeated because you can apply them to many areas of healing and mindset work. It's useful to be reminded of how you can move forward, because often the first time we hear something, we're not fully ready to do the inner work:

- Ensure your vision or dream is powerful enough for you. If you aren't bothered either way about it happening, then why are you wasting your energy on it? Never focus on someone else's definition of success or happiness, this is about you and what you want from life.

- Create an action plan for the next week, month, quarter or year? If you don't know what you're working towards, then how can you achieve it. Maybe you want to take the family away for a holiday, or buy a new home. Once you know your goal, you can break it down into actionable steps, for example saving a little every month or researching locations.

- Have an accountability buddy, which could be a friend, trainer, therapist or life coach. When you're accountable to someone, we're much more likely to take action. Remember what I shared about procrastinating and getting this book completed. Once I had accountability, I got everything done in three months.

- Break your old habits. This can be more challenging that it sounds, because habits often make us feel comfortable and it keeps life predictable and so we can be reluctant to break habits.

- Begin to reflect on what you're really trying to achieve by the things you do and say. The best way to describe this is stepping outside of yourself and looking in. You're trying to see yourself from a neutral perspective and to be curious about the underlying drivers in your choices. Be prepared that you might have to ask yourself some tough questions and this can bring up feelings you don't want to tackle. This is why working with someone can be very useful, they aren't afraid to ask you those questions, because they don't have the same emotional attachment to them.

- If you recognise that you're about to self-sabotage, count to ten, or leave the room before you speak, act or make a decision. Give yourself some space.

- If you find yourself self-sabotaging, don't judge yourself. Just know that you can choose differently next time. This takes an immense amount of pressure off you.

- Take a break from everything and everyone. Sometimes you just need space, to think, to be and to let your body heal. Especially if you've been over working, or have dealt with something a life changing event. When you push yourself too hard, your energy becomes fragmented, so push the reset button. Focus on self-care and get yourself back to a place where you're energised, motivated and clear on the next steps for you.

- Use energy clearing modalities to help you increase your level of self-awareness and to have what you need to move past the sabotaging behaviours. My favourites are things such as EFT/Tapping, Reiki, Meditation and Breath Work. The key, as I've repeatedly shared, is ensuring the modality resonates for you and the practitioner holds a safe space for you.

- Forgive, forgive and then forgive some more. This is both for yourself and for others. Carrying around old emotions such as anger, hurt, resentment and betrayal is exhausting, and it blocks you from moving forward. Forgiveness work can be done in many ways, so chose a modality that works for you. We'll be exploring letting go and forgiveness in the next chapter.

- Know that you deserve more. Release the blocks to feeling worthy and deserving. If this still feels hard for you, revisit those earlier chapters and go back over the exercises to see if there is something you've not yet identified, or let go of.

- Stop focusing on doing the stuff that doesn't really matter and the thoughts that distract you. Ask yourself if your choices and actions are taking you closer to your dreams or away from them. This will help you to stop wasting time on the things that don't matter.

There has been lots to think about in this chapter, so as we bring the topic of self-sabotage and upper limiting to a close, just ask yourself:

1. What could you commit to immediately and begin to do differently to break this cycle of self-sabotage?
2. Do you need support in making this happen?

To finish this chapter, I just want you to ask yourself how many years you're willing to live a half-life, before you'll finally commit to yourself and decide that you deserve better. The sad fact is that many people will stay stuck in a meaningless life rather than commit to healing and taking action. There are people I speak with where I know we'll be having the same conversation in twelve months' time, and then probably in twenty-four months' time. Don't be like them. Don't waste your precious life.

I wrote this book for those who really do want to choose happiness for themselves, they just needed some support and guidance along the way. As with everything new, there is a certain amount of muscle flexing and growing that needs to take place. You don't go to the gym on the first day and expect to walk out without your muffin top and with a six pack instead, although if you find that gym, I want to know about it. The more you commit to understanding yourself and your habits and the more you put the tips into practice, the bigger the transformation will be in your life.

Whatever your underlying reason for not taking action, I'm here to tell you that you always have been, and always will be enough. You just need to remember who you are and start believing in yourself again. Your happiness is waiting.

Chapter 6

Letting the past go, so you can create your future

"The truth is, unless you let go, unless you forgive yourself, unless you forgive the situation, unless you realize that the situation is over, you cannot move forward." Steve Maraboli.

Everything we have looked at so far in this book has brought us to this point;
the way you look at the world, your self-esteem, your fears and your sabotaging behaviours. All of these things have shaped and created your past. The question is, do you want these things to shape your future?

Until you can let of the negative emotions and energies from the past, you'll struggle to create the life you really want. It's such a common way that we keep ourselves stuck and in a state of limbo, because either we don't know how to release the past, or we're simply choosing not to let it go. I firmly believe that we can choose our emotions. Yes, it's hard sometimes, but the freedom to choose our thoughts, which then impacts how we feel, is always available to us.

You'll know if you're struggling to let go because common emotions for you will be anger, resentment, fear, hatred, guilt, shame, sadness, disappointment and the need to control everything in your life. These heavy emotions show you, that you're not accepting your current reality, because your mind is still replaying the past and what you've experienced. The danger with this, is that no matter how much you try and move forward with life, it can be incredibly easy to slip back into old patterns and habits that you thought you had dealt with and released.

In those moments, you might ask yourself what happened, especially with all the inner work you've been doing and your commitment to change. It can feel so infuriating and confusing to find yourself dealing with the same struggles and emotions repeatedly, no matter how much time and energy you've expended on doing inner healing. What I see most frequently with people is that the real root cause of their behaviour, fear, or thinking was never identified and dealt with. Which means they've never truly had the opportunity to release and let go.

Identifying the true root cause, can often be like finding a needle in a haystack, because when we do the inner work, there will always be things that bring some level of peace and resolution to you. Consequently, making you feel better. In those moments you truly believe, or wanted to believe, that you were healed, fixed, or had finally identified the thing, and so could now move on with life. The trouble is feeling a little better and taking the edge off things, is like placing a band aid over a gaping wound, it won't hold for long and those old emotions will always catch up with you.

When you begin to look inwards at what is really going on and someone's reluctance to let go, it's very common to uncover some deeper benefits and psychological reasons associated with not moving forward. To anyone else they may not seem like sensible, good or even valid benefits and reasons, but for the person who is desperately holding on, they're like a safety net to them. They're choosing to feel safe over everything else, because feeling safe, at a very basic level, means surviving. Remember how we talked before about our mind being very dramatic when it wants to be.

I'm sure you're curious as to what things could impact your inability to release the root cause and what could be going on at a deeper subconscious level, so let me share what I see most often.

- If you have feelings of being unworthy of love and you believe you're unlovable, it can be much harder to let go of people who really have no place in your life anymore. The fear of being alone and of never being loved again, makes you tolerate situations and people that most others would have walked away from. You could also believe that this friendship/relationship is the best you could get and therefore it's better to stick with what you have and know. With people who question their worth, the process of releasing and letting go, takes months and years longer than it really should. Sometimes it can even be brought to a head by something unexpected, for example an unforgivable action or choice of words.

- If you're someone who needs to feel in control, or have control in your life, it can feel terrifying to let go. The process of letting go means relinquishing control and handing over your power to someone, or something outside of yourself and choosing to trust. Whether this is about trusting that others really do have your best interests at heart and will be there for you, or that it's safe to surrender to the flow of life, even when you don't always understand all the twists and turns along the way. This is a huge thing to face and to do, if you've always shaped your life and your personality around being independent, strong and always in control of things.

- If you finally release the things that have been holding you back, you'll have to become that new version of you. Your entire identity will shift, and this can feel very uncomfortable as you find out who you really are without the baggage from the past. It could lead to new choices, difficult conversations, letting people go, expansion and growth and facing more than you feel ready for. It can often feel easier and safer to stick with a life that feels familiar and this means holding onto emotions that really have no place in your life anymore.

- When you choose to let something or someone go, there will be feelings of grief and loss that might arise. We often associate grief and loss with bereavement, when in fact it's so much more than that. Grief is anything where we've experienced a change or a loss to something that feels familiar and is comfortable to us. When you think about grief and loss in this way, you can see how every person alive would be impacted by it to some degree. It would include things such as the loss of a friendship, job, marriage, experiencing miscarriage, moving or losing a home, coping with the loss of physical health and even having to accept that your dreams and expectations for the future may not look as you had hoped.

In feeling confident to let go, we need to come to a place of acceptance and surrender to what is, but even the word surrender can have huge resistance attached to it. The *Merriam-Webster Dictionary* definition of surrender is:

- to agree to stop fighting, hiding, resisting, etc., because you know that you will not win or succeed
- to give the control or use of (something) to someone else
- to allow something (such as a habit or desire) to influence or control you

Taken literally, these are powerful statements, and for many they will bring up lots of strong emotions. When I tentatively suggested letting go of anger to a client who was dealing with the heartbreak of infidelity, it felt like an impossible task to them. To release the anger made them feel weak and powerless in the situation. The anger was also providing the perfect distraction from the true pain they were feeling. They knew that looking at their fear of being unlovable and of not being enough was simply more than they could handle. They chose to stay with anger, and they decided not to let go. I'm not even sure to this day if they've let go, but while I know it would help them move on, it's not my choice to make. We all have free will when it comes to choosing the path of our life and in choosing happiness.

Even though the thought of surrendering can make you feel weak, it's actually one of the most powerful things you will ever do. In those moments you're allowing yourself to release emotional pain and instead you're choosing inner peace and calm. You're trusting and having faith that life has a better plan for you and you're opening yourself up to having everything you've ever wanted. For some, this can feel pretty scary, because as mentioned already, your whole identify will have to shift. There will be a complete death and rebirth.

When we think about letting go, it can be easy to focus on the bigger things in life, but it's also really important that we don't forget to let go of the smaller things too. These are the things that irritate and trigger us and become compounded over time, but because they seem small and silly, we choose in that moment to suppress our emotions. Suddenly we find ourselves exploding at something very small and meaningless. In reality this was just lots of small things that we had tried to ignore or pretend didn't matter. We had reached our limit and that last comment, stupid choice by another, or situation we had to deal with, pushed us over the edge. No matter how big or small something seems, it's important that we still make the conscious choice to deal with it and then let it go.

There are a few key areas which are essential to explore as part of the letting go process and we'll look at each one in turn. Just be aware, that this is where you could come up against a lot of internal resistance. If you're questioning if you're truly ready to let go, or if you can even do this, just think back to the question from an earlier chapter, *'What can I no longer tolerate in my life'*. All the motivation and inspiration you need is right there. Feel into the pain of a life where nothing changes, where every day is a struggle and you feel cut off from who you really are and why you're here.

Remember, if you choose to read through this book and not change a thing, then every day is likely to look and feel like today. If you're lucky the monotony will be broken up with a few good moments here and there, but is this enough for you? Is this really what you want? Too often I see people choosing to play the victim and they waste their precious life. Time is the one thing that we're all running out of and the one thing that we can never get back. Choose to free yourself from the shackles you've placed around your own ankles and enjoy every moment of your precious life. It's time to let go and free yourself from the past and I'm right here supporting you.

We'll begin by exploring some key areas to be aware of when it comes to letting go and then I'll ask you some questions, inviting you to reflect on your own life. At the end of the chapter, I'll share some practical tips and tools for moving forward. As we go through these next few sections, just notice what thoughts arise and where you're still holding onto the past. You'll know if you haven't truly let go because those old emotions and feelings will still be present, you may even feel a shift in your body, for example, a tightness in the chest, tension in the shoulders, a sinking feeling in your tummy.

Letting go of old beliefs

We started looking at limiting beliefs in an earlier chapter and if you're still struggling with your own limiting beliefs, then I want you to go back and review this chapter again, because these stories and restrictions are stopping you from moving forward in life.

Like most people I had a number of limiting beliefs that I needed to address and let go of. One of the biggest beliefs that impacted me until only very recently, was that success and being classified as successful, was defined by having a high income and through high achievement. Taking it one step further, achieving success meant I was worthy of love. Even as I type that I know it sounds crazy, but unfortunately, I'm not alone in this belief and that's why it's so important to shed light on this and to talk about it. Many over achievers and perfectionists are simply trying to gain the attention, love and approval of a parent and even though they're now adults, they're still seeking external validation and approval. It's scary how much these childhood beliefs can impact us and the choices we make as adults. It affects not only the way we live our life and our relationships, but also our career and business success as well.

Like many others who have this belief, I was obsessed about all the things I needed to change and improve in my life. The more I stayed stuck in my head, thinking about everything, the longer my list became. It didn't help that I was a recovering perfectionist and hated the thought of being a failure and messing up. One more reason that people might choose not to like or love me.

Battling with this belief meant that I would often make decisions that didn't feel in complete alignment with who I was, or the business I wanted to create. It was too easy to look to the next book, course or expert to help me, so that I could finally experience the achievement and income I so desperately wanted. When I look back, I can't believe how trapped I was in this belief and how nothing was ever enough. I had built a thriving business that more than replaced my corporate income and I was helping thousands of people in the process, but all I could focus on was achieving the elusive six figure income. Somehow that would mean I had made it. I was successful and I was finally enough.

Having such a focused drive, meant I would give energy to things that really didn't deserve my attention and focus, but I couldn't stop chasing that old definition of success. I was not a quitter and a subconscious part of me believed that if you started something, you completed it and saw it though, even if it wasn't right and made you unhappy.

I also believed that you should always listen to people who were seemingly more successful and considered experts in their field. In doing this I had forgotten how to listen to myself and what brought me joy, because I was too busy implementing new strategies and chasing the promise of bigger success. I was exhausted, overwhelmed, unfulfilled and still living in the past. In time I used these feelings as an excuse to not take enough action, or sometimes any action at all. I was burnt out and had nothing left to give. This made me feel even worse about myself, because I knew I had a greater calling and people to help, yet I was stuck playing small and going around in circles chasing what I thought was important.

In letting this go, the most significant thing I did, was to release my childhood definition of success. Instead I decided that success was being happy, healthy and fulfilled by my work. It meant I could focus on just being me and doing work that I love. I had nothing to prove to anyone because I was already enough, and I could finally make decisions that brought me more joy, happiness and inner peace. I could also run my business in a way that felt right and aligned for me, knowing I was exactly where I was meant to be. Through changing my definition of success and my belief about who I needed to be, I found the real me again and I found happiness. Interestingly I also began to earn a lot more money with ease, because I was being true to who I was and the desperate chasing of money and success was gone.

After changing my definition of success, I committed to continually working on my mindset and all the stories that told me I wasn't enough. I started to listen to my intuition again and made choices that felt right for me. I also stopped comparing my journey to that of others. This was so freeing, because as we all know there is always someone further ahead and earning more. I trusted that I would get there when the time was right, but for right now enjoying life and being happy was my priority, I had already sacrificed too much of the present moment.

As you can see, I had a lot to let go of, but in doing the inner work that I've shared throughout this book and in staying committed to myself, I completely changed my life for the better.

Letting go of the past

In this section, I'm referring to all the things that we've ever experienced or been a part of, whether we had a choice in them or not. These situations can be both positive and negative, but if they hold us hostage to a time that no longer exists, then we can be prevented from moving forward in life.

When we're holding onto the good old days, or when things used to be easier, we choose suffering. This is because we've decided that the present is lacking in some way and so is therefore failing to meet our expectations and dreams. We may have spent hours imagining what life would look like, based on our experience in the past, and when the reality is different from the dream, we feel cheated, disappointed, or let down by life. We remember how things used to be and how we used to feel, and we struggle to accept that things are different now.

A classic example of this is making the transition into parenthood. When life becomes challenging and you can't remember the last time you were able to do something for yourself, or even had time to think, you could feel frustrated, trapped and controlled. Even though you may have chosen this path, your life is all about other people who constantly need you and this can be hard at times. All you can think about is a time when life was easier, when you felt free and unrestricted. You may crave excitement, adventure and just time alone and even begin to resent all your new responsibilities.

This is totally normal by the way and after working with hundreds of mums over the years, I hear the same things all the time and honestly, I've felt it myself too. When you continually try and fight what is, you'll end up exhausted and miserable. It's much better to let go of the life you once had and focus on living the one in front of you. One of the best pieces of advice I can give here, is ask yourself what is missing from your life now that was present before, and then commit to bringing more of that into your reality now.

While some of us are able to look to the past with fondest and with happy memories, there are unfortunately some who also experienced trauma and found themselves in horrid situations in life. I wish there was something I could say to help you make sense of that and to take away all the pain and suffering, but the reality is you need to find this place of acceptance yourself. Others can support and guide you and help with the healing process, but acceptance and letting go, needs to come from deep within you. I know this is not always easy, but if we want to choose happiness, we also have to choose to let go. Healing from trauma is a very personal journey and so I have no intention of telling you what an acceptable time frame is for healing. What is right for one person is not for another, what works for person, doesn't for another.

Once you've allowed yourself the time to feel into the emotions that come up, and you're ready for closure and acceptance, then it is time to focus on the future again. It's only when we refuse to do the inner work to heal and we replay the unfairness and pain at every opportunity, that we're choosing to be a victim. I know that every part of you wants to scream and shout at me, to say that you never chose to be hurt, betrayed, abandoned, abused or violated and I hear you.

Believe me, I do understand, but if you refuse to let the situation go and you won't seek appropriate help and healing, then you're choosing not to move on from this experience. You're choosing to define who you are today, by something that happened to you in the past. In every moment I believe you have a choice, it's not always easy to let go, but it is possible. You cannot change the past, but when the time is right, you can decide how this impacts you in the future.

Letting go of what you thought life would, or should look like

One of the things I hear a great deal from people is that this isn't what they thought life would, or should look like. They thought they would be further ahead, they would have achieved more, or things would simply look different. For some this is about their work and business, for others it's more connected to their personal life. Ultimately, they're suffering because life doesn't match what they had hoped or dreamed of.

To give you a better idea of what this looks like, here is a list of things that I see people struggle to accept the most:

- Being single/divorce/separated when you thought you would be happily married
- Having a partner who's not what you hoped for, or expected
- Dealing with relationships challenges
- Not having children yet, or perhaps being unable to have children/more children
- Having children who struggle with illness, or having children who don't meet your expectations when it comes to personality, educational attainments and behaviour
- Not living in your ideal home, or in your ideal location
- Not achieving the success in your business, or in your work that you expected
- Having your freedom and choices restricted, especially in light of the 2020 Coronavirus situation
- Having to adapt the way you work or do business, due to external influences and restrictions.
- Having poor physical health

Over the last ten years I think I've been affected by most of these and because I didn't know how to let go and accept my reality at the time, I experienced a great deal of suffering and numerous physical health issues. I probably annoyed the hell out of those closest to me too, because I would constantly be talking about it. I was trying to process what my life looked like and why it looked the way it did, because at times it just made no sense to me.

One of the things that I shared at the start of this book, was going through a great deal of anxiety and stress in my corporate job. I truly believe that the stress impacted my ability to fall and stay pregnant with my second child and this situation consumed me. I had a very clear vision of having more than one child and because I fell pregnant so easily first time around, I naively thought the same would happen for my second pregnancy.

With each passing month of failing to get pregnant and then two miscarriages at twelve weeks, it's fair to say that falling pregnant was all I could think about. At that time, I had no idea how much of a strain stress and fear for the future can place on your body. This is when I sought out Kinesiology, because even back then I was into alternative solutions. Within one month I had fallen pregnant and this time I stayed pregnant. It was truly a miracle for me. Hence why I knew I had to train in this modality myself and so my new path as a healer began.

I'm a big believer in the mind body connection, because I see it with clients all the time and sometimes I wonder how many people would be spared from illness, if they could just let go. The emotions that they hold onto cause dis-ease in the body, and then balance and harmony becomes hard to achieve. This is when physical symptoms can start to appear. I'm not sharing this to frighten you, I'm simply sharing my experience of working with hundreds of clients over the last few years and my own experience of the mind impacting the body.

I hope you're beginning to think about how your own expectations have stopped you enjoying life and moving forward, because I really want these words to change the way you see everything and to intensify your desire for change.

Letting go of people

There are three separate things to explore when it comes to letting go of people and we're going to look briefly at each of them. It could be that one particular scenario is very relevant for you right now, or you could be struggling with all three. It's good to have an understanding and appreciation of all three, because I'm sure that each will be relevant at some point in your life:

- Accepting that certain people are no longer in your life
- Releasing your expectations of what others should say and do
- Forgiving others for what they have said and done. Which is actually something we'll talk about more later in the chapter

Accepting that people are no longer in your life can be hard to deal with, especially if you had no choice in that person leaving your life. Bereavement and grief are strong emotions to deal with, but there comes a time when you need to remember and honour all the amazing memories of your past together and begin to look to the future again. It's completely right that you would allow yourself the time to feel into these emotions, and to express how you feel. The key thing is not to become trapped in the cycle of healing and dwelling on your loss, because this is when it becomes unhealthy. As I've already said, there are no guidelines for how long it takes to grieve and it's different for everyone, but maybe the telling sign is that you constantly feel stuck and you tend to replay memories of the past.

If we truly want to choose happiness and flow in life, then we have to accept change as part of this. The natural circle of life is that people will continually come into and then out of your life, nothing ever stays the same. We would not try and stop the flow of a river, or the changing of the seasons, this would seem ridiculous to us, but yet we often waste energy on fighting this same flow when it comes to people. We have all seen people who desperately try and cling on to others, they can't accept that it's time to walk away or let the other person go with love. They're fighting against the natural flow of life. When you can lovingly accept that people will enter your life and leave at exactly the right moment, the struggle ends.

I think most of us would openly admit that we have expectations of how we think other people should behave, or how we want them to behave. When they don't meet our expectations, we suffer and create all these stories and meanings around what has happened. We might believe they've betrayed us, let us down, they don't respect and appreciate us, or they don't love us. It can bring up intense emotions such as anger, resentment and sadness.

Think about the parent who desperately wants their child to behave well, or to go to sleep on time. Or the person who is desperate to receive an acknowledgement of love from their partner and believes true love is expressed is a very specific way. This even extends to how you expect friends and clients to behave too. When their actions and choices don't match our expectations, our thoughts can spiral.

I'm sure you're already starting to think about where you're trying to control the behaviour of another and are suffering because it doesn't meet your expectations or what you hoped for. Sometimes we just need to loosen the reins and allow people to be who they are without judgement or expectation. Having this new level of self-awareness, can be a complete game changer in our relationships.

Forgiveness is something that we'll be looking at in more depth shortly, but I know that for many people, they fear that by forgiving someone, they're actually letting them off the hook. That somehow, what they said or did was now acceptable and I want you to know, this is not the case at all. Forgiveness is about letting the person go so that you no longer carry around the heavy emotional and energetic burden associated with them.

There is a beautiful quote from *Budda*, '*Holding onto anger is like drinking poison and expecting the other person to die*'. The anger only harms you. The other person has often moved on, completely oblivious to how you're feeling and many times not even caring.

Exercise

Before we move onto forgiveness and explore the topic more deeply, I just want to ask you to take a moment to really reflect on what you've read about letting go and ask yourself the following questions. Capture any insights in your journal and in the last part of this chapter, I'll share numerous ways you can begin letting go and forgiving. As with any healing, it is always a process and a journey:

1. Are there any limiting beliefs and stories that you know you still need to let go of? If so, then ensure you revisit the earlier chapter on beliefs.
2. Ask yourself where you look back at the past with nostalgia and a sense of loss, wishing that things could be easier. What specifically are you missing in your life now? Identify the things that you would like more of and could implement into your life now? These things could be added to your action plan.
3. Where are you constantly reliving traumatic experiences? Do you need to seek expert support and guidance to deal with your emotions and what has happened to you? Some things we can process and deal with alone, but often the bigger things require help, support and guidance from an outside source or professional. Don't be afraid to ask for help.
4. What are you struggling to accept about your present situation and why? Is there a gap between what your life looks like right now and what you thought it would look like? What steps can you put in place to get closer to your dreams? Again, these can be added to your action plan.

5. Are you struggling to let go when it comes to people in your life? Think about everything from bereavement, to loss of relationships, friends, breakdown of family relationships and peers/colleagues. Can you identify what needs to happen for you to have closure?

Please give yourself enough time to really reflect here before racing on, because it's your commitment to self-awareness and change that will alter your life and your emotional state.

Forgiveness

'The weak can never forgive. Forgiveness is the attribute of the strong'. Mahatma Gandhi.

Interestingly this topic can be a huge blind spot for people. You may say that you've forgiven a person or moved on, but the telling thing is when the story, or the person keeps coming up in conversation. It can also be evident when your reaction to an event is completely out of proportion. These are classic signs that you're still holding onto emotions connected to the past.

So many people battle with forgiveness, so don't feel like you're alone with this. We struggle to let go of the injustice we've experienced and the feelings that another person, or situation evoked for us. That horrible sense of being powerless, worthless and not deserving of respect. We remember all too well the pain we felt and there's a fear that if we just let it go, if we choose forgiveness, the other person could hurt us again.

Forgiveness does not have to be about the other person and making them feel better, or even excusing their actions. It's deciding that forgiveness is the best option for you, because it reflects who you are as a person, how you want to live your life and how you want to feel. When you look at what needs to be done in your future, you may even decide that the most self-respecting thing you can do is to remove this person from your life, or certainly limit your contact with them. Whatever you decide, you're doing this from a place of self-love and what is right for you, it's not about keeping other people happy.

I know this might be hard to process and accept, but forgiving is about expressing the highest possible love for yourself, and for reminding you who you want to be in this life. Don't allow others to take you off course, or dim your light, because the world will miss out on so much if you do. We each influence and impact many people throughout our lifetime, and I have made a commitment to myself to ensure that these moments and experiences are loving, accepting and inspiring. This means I commit to doing forgiveness work regularly.

When we struggle to let go of the hurt and pain that others have inflicted on us, we can experience a substantial decline in our emotional well-being. Depression and anxiety have become far too common in today's society and for many this comes from being unable to forgive others. They carry these old emotions around like a heavy ruck sack, replaying the past over and over. Our mind is so powerful and when emotions take hold, it can't distinguish between what is real now and what was experienced in the past. This means that even conversations and events from years ago are impacting your emotional and physical well-being today, if you keep replaying them in your mind.

Being able to shed all of those low-level emotions is no doubt the aim for us all and I understand that in reality, it can be hard. In choosing to keep these negative emotions alive, you've given your power away. You've given control of your life to something outside of yourself and in every moment, you're being defined by someone else and your past. The person who caused you pain, as you already know, will often have moved on with their life without a second thought about you and their actions. Those negative emotions held tightly in your ruck sack, attack only you, no one else.

If you've consciously chosen a more spiritual path and desire inner peace, then there is nothing that keeps you further from this path, than the inability to forgive. Anger, rage, resentment, disappointment and many other such emotions affect our ability to be fully in the present moment feeling joy, love and gratitude. It also impacts your ability to trust in life and hold onto the knowing that you're exactly where you're meant to be.

I'm going to say this again because it's so important and I really want you to take this in. It's essential and absolutely right to feel into your emotions and admit how you feel, even if you only do this with yourself. Suppression and denial is never healthy in the long run, but once you've moved through this stage of healing, it's essential to focus on living life again and moving forward.

I'm sure for some of you, it will be very clear and obvious about the people you need to forgive, but in case you're not sure, here are some signs that you're holding on and you need to let go:

- Feeling anger, resentment, bitterness or a sense of betrayal and disappointment when you think of that person

- Replaying scenarios and conversations repeatedly in your mind

- Wanting revenge and for them to experience the hurt you went through

- You can't seem to move forward in life no matter what you do, it feels like you take one step forward and then get dragged back two

As you read through this part of the book, I really want you to be honest with yourself in terms of where you're harbouring negative thoughts and feelings towards another. I'm not saying that they weren't and aren't deserved, I just want you to think about the way life will always look if you continue to hold onto these feelings. Can you imagine feeling this way your entire life? Do you really want the other person to have that kind of power and control over your happiness? Too many unhappy people are unable and unwilling to forgive, but I know you want to be happy and you want to choose happiness, so stay open to forgiveness, because this is the path to achieving that.

To better understand why it can be hard to forgive another, let me share some benefits associated with holding onto those negative emotions. It might help you to appreciate why this process can be so hard. Not all of these examples will resonate for you and some may feel like a hard thing to admit to, but know that what comes with honesty and clarity is the chance for emotional freedom.

- You feel with all your heart that the other person doesn't deserve forgiveness. Their actions may have changed the course of your life forever, so why should you forgive and pretend that their choices and actions are now okay. In these situations, you're holding onto the belief that in some way your lack of forgiveness is punishing them, but as we've mentioned before, often they're oblivious.

- For many people, the emotion of anger is very powerful and there is a certain energy to it. They use this energy as something to motivate them in taking action, the anger fuels them. They fear that if the anger is not there anymore, they'll procrastinate or simply won't take any action at all. There is nothing wrong in using the initial energy of anger to get you back into a place of taking action and moving forward with life. You just have to be mindful of how long you choose to hold onto that energy and the actions that you're taking. For example, are your actions constructive or destructive? I know for me personally, if someone tells me I'm not capable of doing something, or doesn't think I'm good enough, I go all out to prove them wrong. The anger creates a fire in my belly, and I use this as motivation to create and achieve. With all the inner work I've done on myself, I'm now able to let go of any negative feelings towards the other person very quickly and instead thank them for giving me the motivation I needed to take action. This energy makes me think of those amazing weight loss stories where people felt so angry and hurt by the cruel comments, that they turned everything around and they now have a body they feel proud of.

- For some people they use the energy and motivation of anger to take revenge. It's the justification they give themselves for retaliating and before you know it, everything has spiralled out of control. The sad thing is that despite all the retaliation, they still feel hurt, let down and disappointed. Was the revenge worth it? If you find yourself wanting to seek revenge, take a moment to ask yourself what you're really trying to achieve. Are you lashing out because you want them to feel the hurt they inflicted on you? Are you trying to teach them a lesson? Get clear, because choosing a more positive way to channel your emotions, will feel better in the long run and you're less likely to hurt yourself and another in the process.

- You enjoy and get benefits from being a victim. The injustice of it all almost gives you permission to moan, complain and to not move forward with your life and it can justify behaving in a certain way. While you think you have a great excuse for not taking action or choosing to be mean, critical and cruel to others, the only person you're kidding is yourself. Not only are you keeping hold of destructive emotions which impact your emotional and physical well-being, you're also choosing powerlessness. Ask yourself what benefits you might be getting by taking on the role of being a victim. Does reliving the story over and over, get you plenty of attention? Perhaps this need for attention is something you've craved your entire life and finally you feel important to others as they listen to you and empathise with you. The trouble is people will get fed up of hearing the same stories repeatedly. If they can't make you stop re-living all this, they will either stop seeing you, or limit the time they have to spend with you. You could end up pushing away the very people you want more attention from.

- By choosing to play the victim you also don't have to face those painful emotions and feelings. Anger is always a mask for something deeper, but to reveal that takes vulnerability and courage. Think about the person who is in fact so hurt and sad by the actions of another, but won't allow themselves to explore their true feelings. Anger they can deal with, but the sadness is just too much. To forgive someone, can mean that you actually have to feel into those emotions of sadness and heartache, and they're terrified by what they might feel and how out of control it could make them.

- By holding onto the anger towards another, you feel as if you have the power in the relationship. All relationships are built on dynamics and we get used to the roles we play in them. If you've always felt like the underdog, who is continually people pleasing and compromising, then having the other person seek your approval for a change can be refreshing. You feel empowered by not giving your forgiveness to them and you finally feel in control. The bigger piece here is about reassessing your boundaries and asking yourself if this is even a healthy relationship for you to be in. Perhaps you need to start speaking your truth and lovingly asserting your own boundaries. If the other person is not willing to truly hear you and respect your boundaries, you can choose to lovingly let them go and move on with life.

- You're angry at the time and energy wasted on that person, and how your trust in people is now completely broken. You're struggling to ever see a time when you could let someone else into your heart again. You fear that letting go of the hurt and pain, could make you vulnerable. That you'll forget what you went through, how much it hurt and how long it took to recover and then you risk having your trust and heart, broken all over again.

In case you're really struggling with the thought of forgiveness, just remember that those negative emotions and feelings are controlling your ability to be happy. Do you really want to give your power away like that, or are you ready to take back control of your life and emotions?

I'm sure there are lots of thoughts coming up for you and it's normal to feel resistance. Don't worry, you still have a little more time in this chapter, before I invite you to start the process of forgiveness and share some tools on how to actually do this. For now, just start to think about the people you might need to forgive and why you haven't been able to so far. Don't forget to place your insights in your journal.

Self-forgiveness

The final part of looking at forgiveness, is self-forgiveness and it's often an area that's overlooked. When we think about doing forgiveness work, we instantly start thinking about all the people who have wronged us or brought us pain, and we forget to look within ourselves. Self-forgiveness is such an essential part of the letting go process, because we need to come to a place of peace with our past choices. Those choices and actions have made us who we are today and brought us to this very moment in time. It doesn't mean we have to be defined by those choices going forward, but we do have to accept what has shaped us.

While forgiving another is hard, we're often able to find it in our hearts to move past the pain. Either we don't want to lose the other person from our life, or we choose to make inner peace more important. When it comes to our self however, we seem to be more blocked and resistant to forgive. We choose instead to punish ourselves repeatedly and we can even seem to gain something from reliving the choices we made, or the action we took.

Much of this can be subconscious. It's certainly not something we spend time dwelling on day to day and it's not usually something that comes up in normal conversation either. Often there's a great deal of shame attached to our past decisions or actions and these are not things that you can talk about with just anyone. So instead we tend to suppress and even deny how we feel, believing that we're completely at peace with what we said and did. Some people will even push the memory so deep, it's like it never happened.

I hope that by reading these words and starting to explore this topic, that old emotions and memories are coming to the surface. Please don't brush over these memories, they're coming into your awareness for a reason. For some of you, it can be very uncomfortable to relive those old memories, but this is your opportunity for growth and healing. You've punished yourself long enough and it's time to express some self-compassion and to finally allow these memories to surface, before deciding to let them go.

The signs that you need to forgive yourself can be different for everyone and they can also be very similar to other emotions that you're struggling with, but as a guide; negative self-talk, self-sabotaging your happiness, success and wealth, your body attacking itself with physical symptoms and illness, or replaying situations and conversations, wishing for a different outcome. It's why self-awareness and the willingness to explore what you feel is so important. It's within that self-exploration, that you'll begin to understand where your emotions are rooted and what they're really about.

In the same way there are many reasons we would choose not to forgive another, there are also several reasons we would choose not to forgive ourselves. So read on and see if any of these ring true for you:

- You've decided that the choice or action you took does not deserve forgiveness. No one else is there to punish you, so you've committed to punishing yourself. If this is you, then you need to let this go. We all make mistakes, but we all deserve a second chance. Have the confidence to know that should a similar situation arise again, you would handle it very differently.

- You've spent your whole life living by certain rules and when you feel as if you've broken your own rules, you struggle to forgive yourself. Neale Donald Walsh says that betraying our self is the highest betrayal of all. Many of us struggle with this, because somewhere within us, we know this statement is true. Just ask yourself who's forgiveness are you really after? Were these ever your rules, your values, or have they been handed down to you from parents, your community, or even by your religion.

- When there is a huge amount of shame connected with your past actions or decisions, it's difficult to explore how you really feel about it, because part of you would prefer to forget and block it from your memory. The danger with denying how we feel, is that we can't see how the emotions are really impacting us. Just because we've suppressed something, doesn't mean it's not driving our subconscious choices.

- We can't stop thinking about how we used our words negatively to attack and hurt another. We see the pain etched in their face and we notice how this negatively impacted the relationship afterwards. The bonds of trust, respect and love are no longer there. We fear we've ruined things and caused irreversible pain to another.

- We didn't respect our boundaries enough and in doing so we didn't respect ourselves. We allowed ourselves to be treated or used in a way that makes us feel insignificant, small and worthless. For example, we didn't speak our truth and express how we really felt, or we didn't do everything in our power to protect another.

- You're holding onto regret and wondering if you should have taken more action, or done something differently. Often this links into not being able to accept how life now looks. If this resonates, you might want to revisit the information earlier in this chapter on letting go.

- When life is not going the way that we hoped and we don't want to take responsibility for decisions and choices we have made along the way, we can choose to blame others, instead of doing the harder self-forgiveness work. We can even believe that they've done this to us, when in fact, we're using them as a distraction and an excuse. We do this because to take responsibility is just too painful. To admit we got it wrong, that we're the ones not stepping up or taking control of our life, is just too much for us to deal with, so we blame those around us. Think about the people you're currently blaming for things in your life, is it time to take your power back, forgive yourself and move on?

How would it feel to decide that today is the day that you're going to forgive yourself and move on? Being able to gift yourself forgiveness and compassion is an amazing thing to be able to demonstrate to others. Be the inspiration that someone else needs, because as you give yourself permission to move forward and be free, you're opening the way for others to do the same.

Exercise

Before we move into the final part of the chapter and the practical tips and tools I want to share with you, just take some reflection time to answer the following questions in your journal:

1. Who do you need to forgive in your life?
2. Why have you been unable to, or chosen not to, until now?
3. Where do you need to forgive yourself?
4. Why have you been unable to, or chosen not to, until now?

If you're struggling to get any insights, or believe this isn't an issue for you, then perhaps try this simple meditation.

1. Close your eyes and take some nice deep cleansing breaths. In through the nose and out through the mouth. Just feel your body relaxing.
2. Let go of the thoughts of the day and give yourself permission to be fully present and set the intention of being open to clarity.
3. Know that you're deeply grounded, imagine roots coming from the soles of your feet and connecting you to the earth if it helps. This is especially useful if you have a busy mind.
4. Know that you're safe, imagine a bubble of energy all around you keeping you safe and supporting you as you go through this process.
5. Ask yourself any questions around forgiveness. For example, who do I need to forgive and why couldn't I before? Where do I need to forgive myself and why couldn't I before?
6. Notice what you see in your mind's eye, and what memories or people appear. Notice any feelings and emotions too.

How to let go of the past and practice forgiveness

The process of letting go and forgiving is a very personal one. What works for one person may not for another. What seems appropriate in one situation, will also not be for another. So have a look at the suggestions below and choose the approaches that resonate and feel right for you.

You may also find that as you read through these suggestions, things pop into your awareness and suddenly you look at people and situations with a new perspective. This is perfectly normal and happens whenever you set the intention for healing. You'll have clarity on where you need to let go and where you need to forgive.

Have your journal and all your insights to hand. Capture any ideas and things you're willing to try. Just note that some examples will be more relevant for letting go and others for forgiveness.

- Get the closure you need. Whether this is clearing out any physical or emotional clutter, or simply putting a stake in the ground. Do whatever gives you the sense that enough is enough, and that you're ready to move on. Closure allows us to release heavy energy that stops us moving forward freely. You can also de-clutter physically. Just think of this like spring cleaning, you're getting rid of all the things you no longer need and creating a more joyful living space. Instead of wading through treacle, we begin to build up our momentum again as everything feels lighter.

- As we've started to talk about already, there can be some benefits of staying stuck. So be honest and ask yourself what benefits you get from not letting go of the past, of not forgiving and of staying stuck. Perhaps you don't have to put yourself out there and face rejection, criticism or judgement. Perhaps you enjoy complaining to your friends or family about how bad things are and you get their undivided attention and for just a few moments the world is about you. When you're clear on the underlying benefits, you can find more positive ways for getting your needs met.

- Surrender and practice detachment from the outcome. Suffering happens when your reality doesn't match your expectations. Stop trying to control everything and allow yourself to be surprised and delighted by who and what enters into your life. Your mind is limited, but the universe is infinite, so let it do its thing.

- Are you expecting the possible? Try and put things into perspective. Being a perfectionist and having high standards can make life incredibly challenging for you and those in your life, so ask yourself if your expectations are realistic? Focus on self-love and being enough already, without having to achieve and do more.

- Know that there's no rush, so slow down and don't be in such a hurry to get there or arrive. Everything happens at exactly the right time, so trust in that and enjoy the present moment. When you judge yourself as going too slow, you will experience anxiety and fear. Life will become about the push, instead of enjoying each moment for what it is and appreciating the world around you. We're all striving to truly connect with who we are, why we're here and to know ourselves just that little bit more. Everything we experience in life takes us closer to this, but it takes time and cannot be rushed, everything happens at the perfect moment.

- Stop comparing yourself to others and what they have achieved, or what you think they would do. Comparison is always a dangerous road to go down, because there will always be someone richer, healthier, slimmer and more successful than you. Just focus on being the best you, that you can be.

- Allow yourself the time and space to feel into the emotions. Don't stay with the anger and the negative, as this is only a mask. Go to the hurt and see what emotions are present. If it makes it easier write it down, or perhaps talk through with a trusted friend or professional. When we choose to be supported by other people, we can get the accountability we need to move forward and truly commit to change. We also benefit from an outside perspective on what's going on.

- If you're ready, look for the learning, just ensure you haven't overlooked how you really feel. What has this taught you, for example, I need to ensure I speak my truth, enforce my personal boundaries, or I need to be kinder and more accepting of myself and others. Look for the gift, because life happens for you and not to you. When you can be grateful for the person you've become and what you now have in your life because of your experiences, it makes it much easier to let go of anger, hate and resentment. For example, how can you hate the body that gave you beautiful children? How can you hate the job that allowed you to buy your amazing home?

- Separate the person from the behaviour, especially if this is someone very close to you, for example, a child or partner. The behaviour may have been bad, but the person as a whole is not. Often their actions speak more about what is going on for them, than about you. Because we experience the hurt, we take it personally, but there are things going on for the other person too. This could be a great opportunity to reconnect and create a better relationship. There is always a choice.

- Accept that in the moment, you made the best decision you could. Looking back maybe you could have chosen differently, but that decision has brought you to exactly this point and made you who you are today. Choose the learning and then know that you have the power to choose differently next time. Taking responsibility will help you to feel more empowered and in control.

- Shining light on the shame by admitting what you did and how you feel and then exploring this with another is very therapeutic. Just ensure you choose the other person wisely, and trust that they will create a safe space for you to explore this and will offer you unconditional acceptance. This is when working with a professional or someone skilled at holding space is essential.

- Choose compassion and self-acceptance, because as we've already discussed, no one is perfect. We're all on a journey and learning to express compassion is part of this journey. Along with forgiveness, it is the thing that takes us closer to feeling inner peace, because in every moment we choose to be more loving and accepting, of ourselves and others. Don't believe the inner voices that tell you that you don't deserve forgiveness or more from your life. To release and forgive try sending love, light and healing to your Heart Chakra. Very simply, you can place two hands over your heart space and breath in through your nose and out through your mouth. Imagine a beautiful white light or energy coming down through your head and heading straight to your heart.

- Just as you would hope that no one would judge you, you need to extend the same courtesy to others. Challenging when it's someone you care about, I know. You desperately want to help and show them a better way, but all that happens is that they get frustrated and annoyed with you. They feel like you're preaching and don't understand them.

Just practice compassion and acceptance for who they are and where they're at in their journey, because this is the ultimate expression of love.

- If you still feel like you need forgiveness, there is always the option of communicating your feelings to the other person. If this isn't possible or appropriate, you could write them a heartfelt letter and then burn it, or even meet soul to soul in meditation. This is where you can express your emotions and ask for forgiveness. It will always be given at soul level, because here there is only love.

- If something or someone has triggered you, count to ten and choose your response. Forget your old patterns and behaviours, choose a more loving response. Ask yourself if you have blown things out of proportion. Will this really matter in one, three, or five year's time? If not, then why are you wasting energy on it now, do you want to be right or happy?

- Use a form of energy healing that resonates for you, for example, EFT/Tapping, Kinesiology, Reiki, Breath Work etc. Sometimes it's difficult to get to the root cause of our emotions alone. We have no idea what we might find when we start digging, so we often avoid the very places we most need to go. Working with an energy healer, gives you the support you need to release old wounds and trauma in a safe way. These practices are also incredibly soothing and healing for the soul.

- Meditation really is a magical tool and it's becoming more popular and more mainstream too. Whichever style you use, it will help you to get back in touch with what is really going on within you and help you connect to who you really are. I always feel such a sense of peace after meditating, there is never any need to control outcomes or others, I can just accept what is. If you go to the end of this book, there are some free resources listed for you to try. There is a beautiful guided meditation for forgiving others and another for forgiving yourself.

- Take action. If there are things within your life that you struggle to accept or that you need to move forward on, the only thing that will change things is action. It's all part of building up your trust muscle again.

I'm sure this has been a powerful chapter for many of you, so don't worry if you've had to stop reading and come back to this before you were ready to move forward. Healing is a journey and you can't fix a lifetime of emotional baggage and pain through reading a book like this once.

With everything you've explored and reflected on so far, what are you ready to move forward with and commit to? Make sure you write this down in your journal and you hold yourself accountable. Remember, nothing in life will change until you do, so commit to change.

Chapter 7

Allowing more into your life

We've reached our final chapter, and this is where everything comes together and you allow yourself to be, do and have more than you ever thought possible. We'll explore what it means to receive, plus you'll understand the importance of taking a holistic approach to your emotional well-being. You'll end this chapter with clarity on what you're ready to commit to and you'll start to create a strategy or plan that works for you in choosing happiness every day.

I know we've covered a great deal in this book and I'm sure that lots of insights have arisen, as well as lots of questions. Just remember that life and inner healing is a journey, we don't just fix and change everything once, because as our inner world grows, expands and evolves, so too must our outer world. To have a life of deep meaning and happiness, we need to constantly choose growth and change and that means continually reflecting on the life we're living and how we feel. If the present is not making us happy, we have the freedom and ability to choose differently. We just have to commit to our own happiness and to doing the inner work.

I know that at times it can feel as if life reflects the exact opposite of what you truly want, despite your commitment to doing the inner work. There is a sense of deep struggle around certain aspect of your life and you just can't seem to manifest the things you truly desire, no matter what you do. I understand this is a source of deep frustration for you, especially as you see others around you attracting things with ease. It makes no sense with all the mindset work and healing you've done. You're tired from the constant push and struggle of life and you have a deep knowing that things should be easier.

So, what is happening? Well, the answer is simple, it's because you're blocking the very things you desire from appearing in your life. I know it may seem ludicrous that you would be blocking the life you so desperately want and I'm sure your natural reaction is to deny this, but what are the other options? That life is unfair, that nothing you do is enough, or that good things just don't happen to you? This puts you in a position of being powerless, are you really sure you want to hold onto those beliefs and sit in that camp?

I've worked with enough people now to be able to see the patterns and of course, I've been there too. The minute that life begins to feel hard, when I know I'm doing all the right things and yet life isn't moving forward, I start looking at where I'm blocking myself and choosing not to receive. I may not always like what I see and of course I get frustrated and cross with myself, but this self-awareness gives me power and strength to choose differently.

Throughout this chapter, I'll help you to become aware of where this applies to you too and I'll give you some techniques to move past this. Plus, I'll be inviting you to create a strategy or plan that works for you and inspires you to take action in making your dream life a reality. Remember, without taking action you risk life continuing as it always has. You deserve to have an amazing life, and I truly believe you're capable of creating it, you just need to get clear, put together a plan and then begin taking action forward.

So, in this final chapter, we going to look at; your willingness to receive and why you could be blocking more from entering into your life, the importance of focusing on self-care and having a holistic approach to your emotional well being and finally I'll invite you to create your plan. As a thank you for trusting me to be your guide throughout this book, I'm also going to share some free resources which will support your healing journey.

Are you willing to receive?

Many of the things we've explored in this book, impacts our ability and willingness to receive. It's what defines our sense of worth and what we think is possible for us. It's why doing the inner exploration and healing is so essential if we want to have a life that brings us happiness. We need to identify and then release all of the negative stories, beliefs, fears and old habits that hold us back and keep us feeling stuck.

If your life doesn't look as you want it to right now and yet you're taking the right action and doing the inner work, then there's a very good chance that you're not giving yourself permission to receive. For many people, they do the inner work, they take action, and the life they desire is finally coming closer, but at the final moment, they don't allow it into their life. I'm sure this sounds ridiculous to you and every part of you will want to deny this, especially if it's connected to something you really want. So often I hear people say, *'but why would I reject money when I really need it'*, or *'why would I be closed off to love, when all I can think about it meeting someone new'*. This is when there is conflict between the conscious and subconscious mind. Just reflect back to the chapter on self-sabotage and upper limiting.

One of the ways to better understand our willingness to receive, is to begin observing our patterns and habits in receiving the smaller things in life. Before we even begin to look at how you receive things like success, happiness, money and love, let's just take some time to review the smaller things that you're faced with every single day. For example, do you find it comfortable to receive a compliment, accept help, or have someone really be present and listen to you? Do you allow yourself to be supported, or do you try and do everything yourself? What about when someone else offers to pay for coffee or dinner, is this difficult for you, or does it feel wonderful to receive this?

I'm sure your mind is already processing and analysing past choices and current habits. You might even be thinking about why it doesn't feel right, safe or natural to receive. We'll explore this in more depth shortly, but it's worth knowing that people with a low self-esteem will often struggle with receiving smaller day to day things. There is a deep-rooted fear that they don't deserve what is being given and they don't deserve more in their life generally. These people are struggling with feeling like they're enough, and knowing that they're worthy of good things happening to them. As you can see, our mind is such a powerful tool at times, but it can also be our greatest enemy.

Is any of this beginning to resonate for you and are you starting to see things that you couldn't before? To help bring this to life a little more, I'm going to share some of the smaller ways we're given the chance to receive every day. Just think about how this applies to you and your natural reaction:

- Compliments. When someone tells you that they like how you look, they admire what you're able to do, or what you've achieved, can you easily receive this feedback? Perhaps your natural reaction in the past has been to push back the compliment, or even reject it. Let's imagine that someone says, *'You look amazing in that'*, your instinct could be to say *'oh no, this old thing. I just found it in the back of my wardrobe'*. Or perhaps you're very gifted in an area of your life and when complimented on your skill and ability you say, *'It's nothing really, anyone can do this'*. A receiving and open response would be to say, *'thank you'*. For some people though, it can be hard to hear the compliment because it contradicts how they feel about themselves and so creates inner discomfort.

- Accepting help. This can be a very tricky pattern to break, especially if you're used to being strong and independent. It can make you feel as if you're failing by not being able to do the task alone, and so often people will choose to struggle over feeling like a failure or weak. There are clearly links to over achievement and perfectionism here and for some the sense that they don't deserve help. A good example would be someone offering to help you complete a task, whether at home or work, and your first reaction, is *'don't worry I can do it'*, or *'thanks but I can manage'*. For some people, trust also comes into play here. They don't believe that other people can be relied upon, or will do it to the standard that they want. It feels easier to do everything themselves and to remain in control.

- Allowing people to be fully present for you. This was my own personal struggle, because having people be fully present for me and really listen to what I was thinking, and feeling was hugely uncomfortable. I would always try and switch the focus of the conversation back to them. For me, I doubted that people were truly interested in me and what I had to say, I questioned the significance of my voice and opinion as it was overlooked so many times. Whatever the reason behind the habit, I was blocking my ability to receive, and this didn't help with the flow of bigger things. Luckily, I now have more self-awareness and insight, I've done the inner work around being heard and receiving now feels much more natural.

- You only want to receive in a certain way, which means you're trying to control what things should look like, when they should happen and how it should come to you. Nothing blocks our ability to receive more, than being overly attached to the process and the outcome. Just think back to everything we explored in the last chapter on letting go. By holding on so tightly, you block your ability to see other opportunities that could be very advantageous, or you struggle to appreciate the things that have come into your life. For example, your partner surprises you with a holiday, but you're not happy. It's to a place that wasn't on your list, it's not the week you wanted to go, and you would have preferred to have chosen the holiday yourself. Ungrateful yes, but also what if this was going to be the best holiday ever and yet because you were closed off to it, you missed out on how amazing it could have been. The same is true of business and work opportunities or finding a new home or partner. If it doesn't look as we've expected or hoped, we don't always allow ourselves to receive and we end up missing out. Day to day, this could be as simple as what you're planning on doing, where you're going, or what's for dinner.

- You're trying to control the actions of others, as you're holding onto expectations for how they should behave. When you refuse to accept people for who they are and you keep hold of the belief that you can change them or control them, you're opening yourself up to lots of heartache and you're missing out on who they really are. There will be so much about them that you can't see and don't receive, because you're too focused on what you want the relationships and their actions to look like. If you don't like who they are and what they stand for, then you have decisions to make. Accept them warts and all, or lovingly release your need to control and change them. Reflect back on everything we explored in the chapter on relationships around boundaries, toxic people and of course the chapter on letting go.

- You overlook what is right in front of you and already present in your life, instead you focus on lack and there not being enough. Earlier in the book we explored how you can choose to look at the world, with a glass half empty or glass half full. If you're more focused on the glass being half empty, you'll naturally see lack everywhere and you'll be unable to appreciate everything that is already in your life. It's likely that you'll focus on a lack of time, money, energy, holidays, sunshine, good things on TV, nice people to spend time with, things to do, support from others and so much more. As discussed in earlier chapters, feelings and emotions seep into all areas of life and so this feeling of lack will be everywhere, and nothing will feel like it's enough for you. In time that becomes your default setting and you'll be blocking yourself from receiving the very things you want. When your natural reaction is one of, not enough, and lack, there will be so much in life that you miss. Just think about simple pleasures; a beautiful sunset, amazing friends and family.

Now that you've identified where you're not allowing yourself to receive, you may be feeling rather confused as to why this is happening. You thought you had done the inner work and were ready for more. This is such a common occurrence for people, so don't be too hard on yourself. Let's explore together a few of the reasons that you may be unable or unwilling to receive. After this next section I'll share some questions with you, that will help you to reflect on everything we've discussed on receiving.

Why you're unable to receive?

We've started to touch on a few of the reasons for this already and we've explored many of these mindset areas earlier in the book. For example, things such as low self-esteem, not feeling worthy of the life you dream of, fear, sabotage, facing an upper limit and the ability to let go. Each of these can impact not only what we think we deserve, but also what we believe is possible. This is definitely a very emotive subject and can cause such frustration for people.

The following are things that I tend to see the most in my clients and things I've had to deal with myself too. If you find yourself resonating with any of these examples, please revisit earlier chapters where we explore things in more depth. There will be something within that area of mindset, that needs more time and attention:

- You don't believe it's possible, because you simply don't know how you can create the life you really want. You have clarity on the end goal or dream, but the steps to making that happen are so unclear for you. You'll often say, *'I don't know how'*, *'I can't do it'*, or *'the dream life feels so big and far way, I just don't know how to get from here to there*'. This makes you feel powerless because you don't have all the answers yet. All the old stories about being enough, being worthy and of needing to let go and trust are arising for you.

- Following on from the first example, you also don't trust in something bigger than you to provide, whether you would choose to call this god, the universe, divinity or source. You've never really considered, or truly believed, that you're not alone and that something bigger than you, is there to support and guide you in creating your ideal life. When we choose to trust in something bigger than ourselves, it doesn't mean you have to be religious; it just means you have to be open to being supported and not doing everything on your own.

- You get what you expect and so life becomes a self-fulfilling prophecy. Have you noticed that some people just expect good things to happen and generally it does? You expect it to be hard and a struggle and so that is exactly what you get. Think back to all those limiting beliefs about what is possible for you and all the ways you sabotage when things get too good. This way of thinking means that you're restricting what is able to come into your life. Your heart is not fully open to receive.

- You have a strong belief that you should be able to make everything happen yourself and allowing others to help and assist makes you weak. It could also confirm the belief that you're not good enough to do things alone.

- You could fear that you're a burden to people and that they don't really want to help you, so it's easier not to ask. Then you avoid rejection.

- When it comes to receiving a compliment, there can be a fear that the other person isn't genuine. They don't really mean what they're saying, and they have an ulterior motive. There is something they want you to do for them.

- You might fear that receiving something from another means your indebted and you'll owe them something. You could feel apprehensive about what the price could be and so it seems easier and safer to reject what they're offering.

- You're holding onto the fear of opening your heart. It could feel scary to have everything you've ever wanted. If this feels true then just revisit the chapter on self-sabotage and upper limiting, there might be something there that needs more attention. You might also be scared that in opening your heart to more, you risk having to deal with some of the things you've buried and denied, or that being open hearted means you're more at risk of being hurt again in the future. It's normal to feel apprehensive, but you have so many tools and so much support in this book. Remember growth comes from being willing to step outside of our comfort zones.

- You're trying to remain in control, because this is the only way you feel safe. Not having the answers and not having clarity makes you feel very anxious, so you keep your world small so that you always feel in control and know what life will look like and feel like. Even if the price is growth.

- You worry that you don't deserve what other people are offering and so you reject the compliment, attention or help.

Exercise

Now that we've looked at where you could be blocking yourself from receiving more and why this is happening, take some time to look at the following questions. Please don't rush through these, because your inability or unwillingness to receive could be the missing piece when it comes to having a life you love.

1. Take a moment to think about how you feel when someone is complimenting you, perhaps think about a recent example. Do I allow myself to open heartedly receive the compliment?
2. Why do I tend to reject the compliment, or push it away?
3. Do I allow others to pay for things for me? If not, why not?
4. How do I feel about accepting help from others? What am I making it mean when someone offers to help me, or when I accept help?
5. Do I feel like I'm in debt when someone does something nice for me? Do I owe them a favour? Is there always a price to pay?
6. How does it feel when people are really listening and interested in me? Think about those moments when people are looking at you, maintaining eye contact and asking questions.
7. Do I like to be in control of things and how does it feel to surrender a little? Am I still attached to the outcome of things and how things must happen? Can you see where your need to control has caused you to miss out on feeling joy and having an appreciation for things as they are? If you're still struggling with letting go and acceptance, then ensure you revisit the previous chapter.
8. Where in life am I still focusing on lack and there not being enough? Again, if you can identify that more inner work needs to be done with this, then please refer back to earlier chapters.
9. Are there any other reasons that it feels so uncomfortable to receive? What are you making the act of receiving mean?

Please don't feel dismayed if you have suddenly realised that there is still more inner work to do. As I keep saying, the more we choose to grow, expand and evolve, the more inner work we'll need to commit to. This book is a resource you can come back to time and again and I guarantee every read through will bring you more awareness of yourself and what's been holding you back.

How to open up to receiving more

I'm sure that with everything we've explored in this chapter so far, you're already starting to see areas of growth. If you want to receive more into your life and you want it to feel comfortable, safe and easy, start small and get practicing. Get used to how it feels and then do more of it. Remember, it's like working a muscle in the gym, it takes time and commitment. Although it will feel uncomfortable and unnatural at first, don't give up, because it will become easier. Soon there'll be no stopping you, it will change how you feel physically and emotionally, and you'll be more open and receptive to good things happening for you.

Many of these suggestions can also be found in previous chapters of the book. Repeating them again here, is a reminder of just how important it is to commit to these simple practices in changing your mindset and your life.

- Graciously accept compliments. Practice saying thank you, even if you find it hard to believe the compliment, accept it anyway. Over time this will become easier for you. Trust that people genuinely mean what they say and have no ulterior motive and want nothing from you in return.

- The next time someone offers help, willingly accept it. Enjoy the process of working together to get something completed. Or simply enjoy the fact that your workload has eased, or your stress and responsibilities have been reduced. You do not have to prove yourself to anyone and you don't need to have everything figured out.

- When the focus of attention comes to you, embrace it. Don't try and immediately shift the attention onto someone else. Start to share a little of yourself, this small shift will have a huge impact on your relationships, because when you open up and become more vulnerable, people feel connected to you. Focus on building a genuine connection with the other person and believe that this is their goal too. You deserve to be seen and heard and your voice and thoughts matter.

- Detach and let go of the outcome. The result will always be whatever is needed and know that even if it doesn't look the way you hoped, that's okay. Sometimes life has a better plan, so trust and go with the flow.

- Let go of control and feeling overly responsible when it comes to other people. There comes a point when you have to let go and accept where others are at in their journey. For those that you choose to keep in your life, appreciate their uniqueness, the way they look at the world and how this has made you grow as a person.

- Practice acceptance with what is and the things you can't change. Trying to change people and circumstances that are out of your control is the definition of madness. When you stop trying to change people and situations, you gift yourself more time and space, because there's less you need to do. You also remove any feelings of conflict and a sense of battling with what is.

- Meditate regularly with a focus on expanding your heart space. This will help you to be more present, to see the beauty of the current moment and to trust in the process of life. With that comes an increased ability to receive, because you're open to the flow of life.

- Stop comparing your life to others. Trust that you're exactly where you're meant to be, and that life is unfolding perfectly. When we can reach that place of acceptance within ourselves, it's much easier to enjoy the journey of life.

- Whenever you can, celebrate. Too often we rush ahead to the next thing that must be completed, or that needs our attention. Stopping and taking the time to celebrate is essential. It's a chance to turn around and reflect on how far we've come and to inject some fun into our lives. So, celebrate all the milestones that feel important, be grateful that they happened and that you got to play a part in them. Anniversaries, birthdays, the holidays, the first time your child walks, a promotion at work, a pay rise, your most successful month ever, the list is endless. The more you choose to celebrate, the more things you will notice that deserve celebration

- Be open to the learning in every situation and be grateful for the growth. When we take this perspective, we become much more open to receive whatever comes our way. We've let go of control and we're allowing every person and situation to be what it needs to be, without our judgement. I know that looking for the learning can take time and practice but think about a challenging situation you've had to deal with in the past, or maybe you're struggling with now. What have you learnt about yourself, or about life as a result of this? Has anything positive come from this experience?

- Practice gratitude whenever you can. When it comes to allowing more into your life, one of the most transformational things you can do is switch your attention from lack and not enough, to being grateful for what you have already. This is not just a nice to do, this is something that has been scientifically proven time and again. The research shows that when you commit to a gratitude practice you ultimately feel happier. Gratitude also helps by giving you more perspective, because things are often not as bad as you think. It enhances your appreciation of what you do have in life and for who others truly are. If you want to try a gratitude practice, then here are some fun ideas:

- Keep a gratitude journal/diary. Start small and every evening list three things that you're grateful for. You'll go to sleep feeling positive which is perfect for a great nights sleep and waking up energised and excited by life. Also, if you know that you'll have to find three things a day to be thankful for, your awareness will improve as you look for things to list. We all know that what you focus on, you get more of, so identifying good things will just help open you up to more in your life. Another bonus to this practice is that once you get into the swing of this you will realise just how amazing your life already is.
- Future gratitude journaling. This is where you write about your day with gratitude and as if your ideal day has already happened. You can write about how incredible it felt to wake up in your dream home, to make coffee in your perfect kitchen, to look out of the window and see your perfect view. You might then talk about your business, your friends and family and all the amazing thing you get to do and have. Allow yourself to get in the feeling of it, as well as describing it.

Personally, I found the shift into receiving more so refreshing and heart opening. It suddenly allowed me to see where life and others were already trying to give to me and support me. With all of the things I've suggested above, my aim is to help you in opening your heart to more and to feel safe in doing this.

The importance of self-care in choosing happiness

I truly believe that good physical health is a key foundational piece of our emotional well-being, so we need to approach it with the respect it deserves. I appreciate that this topic is huge and physical symptoms can be vast and varied, however, it's essential to look at your basic health and where you could be papering over the cracks. All too often we battle with niggling aches and pains, but because it doesn't make us stop, we push on anyway and vow to deal with it when we have time.

To give ourselves the best possible chance of being positive and choosing happiness, we need to start with nourishing and fuelling our physical body correctly. Too many people are offered medication as a quick and easy fix when things aren't quite right, or our mood is low. Often the root of the issue is in the way we care for ourselves.

We all live such busy lives and often, we push our minds and bodies until there is nothing left to give. There is the constant stimulation of social media, of trying to balance home life and work, of trying to be all things to all people and of striving to have it all. At some point the body and mind pushes back and we begin to struggle, we experience low mood, lack of energy and annoying aches and pains. With our delicate nervous systems, we can easily become overwhelmed, exhausted and ill. If we don't have a solid self-care plan, we're leaving ourselves exposed and vulnerable.

Without good physical health, life can become a struggle, our thoughts can be consumed with what is wrong, how to fix it and all the ways that we are now being held back by a lack of good health. We get frustrated because we think our bodies should be able to cope. The one thing I have learnt over the years is that illness is our body's way of trying to get our attention. Physical symptoms and aliments are a clear sign that something is out of balance and needs addressing.

Our biochemistry is a delicate balance, from the gut flora levels in the intestines, to the release of hormones for normal bodily functions. When things are out of balance, boy do we know about it. Rather than stopping and taking the time to listen to what our bodies are trying to tell us; we push through the discomfort and the pain. We feed our bodies junk food and caffeine to force it to do what we need. We push ourselves to the limit, and we refuse to stop, even when we're ill. All of this has a huge impact on our physical and our emotional health and it's compounded over time.

I have tried many times over recent years to be superwomen and to have and do it all, and it just doesn't work like that. Something had to give and for me it was my health. I would keep going and focus on everyone else until my body made me stop and quite honestly it was often a relief. I then had a real reason to stop, a physical aliment that I genuinely felt. I didn't have to come up with a justification about time out for self-care and I didn't have to feel guilty, because my priority was getting my health back on track. I'm now much more mindful of when I'm over doing it. I know when to stop and rest and I also have the confidence that when I return to work, I'll be more intuitive and present for my clients.

Maintaining a good level of physical health is essential in ensuring we feel good physically, that we feel happy and that we have the energy and vitality we need to live a meaningful life. If you want to have an abundant life and feel happy, you need to take care of your body, because this in turn will take care of your mind. It's time to take an honest look at your own health and see if there are some changes that you need to make, because focusing on the mind alone is not enough.

Exercise

The following question are especially important if you're doing all the inner work and yet you're still struggling with energy levels, motivation and clarity. My intention is to get you thinking about some of the most simple and basic things you can do immediately to support yourself in a holistic way. When you look at these questions, please reflect on what works for you, for example just because you know someone who can get by on five hours sleep a night, does not mean you can, or should. Ask yourself:

1. Are you happy with the quality and quantity of your sleep? Everyone is individual and so only you will know how much you need. The suggested amount is approximately 8 hours a night so that you can be performing at your best, play around with this and see what works for you. Symptoms of not having enough sleep, can be feeling irritable, emotional flat or apathetic, moody, poor memory, weight gain, increased blood pressure, stress and a weakened immune system.
2. Are you drinking enough water every day? The amount we each need is very different, because it depends on so may varying factors; your height, weight, how active you are, where you live. As a general guide woman need about 2 litres. Water is the most essential thing for our health and every major system in the body needs water to function. It is used for flushing out toxins from your vital organs, it carries essential nutrients to the cells in your body and hydrates you. Common symptoms of dehydration are; low energy/fatigue, mental fatigue/lack of concentration, headaches, back ache, stress, constipation, reduced urination and when you do go it is yellow or orange and dry and itchy skin.
3. What physical symptoms and aliments have you been ignoring? For example, do you suffer from IBS or any other digestive health issue; think everything from acid indigestion, right through to bloating, diarrhoea and constipation? Do you suffer with stress, anxiety or panic attacks? Do you have an auto immune disorder?

4. Are you eating a balanced and varied diet, including vegetables and fruit? Are you eating foods that do not agree with you, for example; sugar, wheat, gluten or dairy? Do you eat more processed foods than you should? Are you relying on different forms of caffeine to get through the day?
5. Do you regularly exercise and move your body?
6. Do you take time out to relax, to do things such as meditation, yoga, breath work, walking in nature?

Looking at your answers to the questions above, are you still happy with the way you feel physically, or can you now accept that work needs to be done? You need to get honest with yourself, because otherwise nothing will change and there will always be something that you will struggle with. Too many people refuse to give self-care the attention it deserves and it's often the first thing to get ditched when life becomes too busy. Your health is essential for a full and happy life, so take the time to reflect on what you need.

1. Reflecting on the questions above and your answers, what changes need to be made immediately?
2. If you know you need support in this area, what kind of expertise do you need and who could you reach out to?

Create your action plan, free resources and next steps

Whether you've read this book in one go, or you dipped in and out when you needed it, what I'm sure has been clear, is the need to commit not only to doing things differently, but to taking action.

At the end of each chapter, or chapter section in this book, there were questions for you to reflect on and an invitation to take action and choose differently. If you didn't take the time then to get clear on what was needed for you, then please do that now. If you head straight back into life, or you race onto the next book, you're missing the point. It's all about what we will allow ourselves to receive and nothing will change until we commit to ourselves and gift ourselves that time.

I'm sure as you made your way through this book you identified strong patterns in your thinking, your emotions and in what actions you need to take. My advice would be to work out what needs your immediate attention, and what you can commit to over the coming months. To try and do everything at once would be very overwhelming and it's likely you would simply give up.

The first thing I do is get really clear on what I want from every area of my life, just like I invited you to do in chapter one. I picture it in my mind, and I feel it in my body. With this vision as my goal, I then tend to plan the next twelve months. Although my vision is very likely to take more than twelve months, it feels more manageable and achievable for me to break it down in this way. So, this is how I tend to plan:

- What are my priorities are and what time do I have available?
- What actions do I want to commit to immediately?
- What should I plan for during the next three months?
- What are my plans for months three to six, six to nine and then nine to twelve?
- What support or accountability do I need?
- How much money will I potentially need? If you're thinking of doing healing work, attending workshops or courses, you need to be clear about the cost implications and ideally plan for this.

As you reflect on what's needed, you may decide or become aware that you need support. I am always here to offer my support, to share resources and to work with you if you're ready. If you click the link below, you'll be able to access six free guided meditations to support you in your healing journey. They will be delivered as MP3 files straight to your inbox, and they're yours to keep.

https://mariehoulden.com/bonus-meditations-and-resources/

If you know that you would like to have more personal help and support from me, I would be delighted to hear from you. The link below will show you how we can work together in a deeper way.

https://mariehoulden.com/

As we bring this book to a close, I just want to thank you for trusting me to be your guide in choosing happiness. I wish you every success in the future and if you should ever want to let me know about the changes you made in your life, or how this book has helped, please do get in contact:

hello@mariehoulden.com

About the author

Marie is a Mindset Coach, EFT Practitioner and Energy Healer for Sensitive Souls, who has worked with hundreds of people, in thousands of private sessions and workshops.

She works with amazing people like you, who know they're destined for more and are ready to confront the belief that they have no choice but to settle for the life they're living. The only problem is you're feeling overwhelmed and you're running out of energy - emotionally, physically and spiritually. Often your caring nature can feel like a burden and you know you take on too much responsibility for others.

She knows that you're sick of that cruel voice in your head, which fills you with self-doubt and makes you lose faith in yourself and your decisions. You wonder if you're special enough, deserving enough or can even create the life you deeply crave. Releasing your limiting beliefs and facing your fears head on, will help you to silence your inner-critic once and for all.

She wants to help you finally move on with your life, having a strong belief in yourself and your capabilities and with an inner knowing that you can have everything you've ever wanted.

Marie currently lives with her family in the beautiful seaside town of Bournemouth. She is passionate about reading, learning, music, deep and meaningful conversations, camping, being outside and has a real soft spot for dogs and horses. Her favourite way to start the day is with a strong coffee, a thought-provoking book, and cuddles with the dog.

To find out more about Marie, have a look at her website here:

https://mariehoulden.com/

Disclaimer (2020) Marie is a fully qualified Kinesiologist, EFT practitioner, Strategic Intervention Coach, Reiki Master and Transformational Bodywork Practitioner and holds all relevant certifications and insurance relevant to these practices. Marie is not a doctor, registered dietitian, psychotherapist, nutritionist or psychologist. Marie is considered alternative or complementary by Western health care professionals and does not replace conventional or current health treatment. Marie does not provide medical diagnosis, or consultations related to health, medical, or psychiatric issues. It is expected that you will take full responsibility for your own health and well-being. The information contained within this book, is provided to you only as general information. Any information, stories, examples, do not constitute a warranty, guarantee, or prediction regarding the outcome of reading this book.

Acknowledgements

I have so much gratitude for each and every person who has ever trusted me with their energy and emotions. It's truly an honour and a privilege to be part of someone's healing journey. There is nothing that brings me more joy than seeing people achieve their definition of success and happiness.

I would like to extend a special thank you to all those people who encouraged me to get the book completed and not give up. Your support and belief in me will always be remembered.

To Hannah and Joshua Houlden, thank you for being patient while Mummy was finishing the book and working some long hours. Now it's done, we have lots more time for board games and walking our beautiful dog Evie.

Finally, thank you to Martin Houlden of South Design Ltd, who produced my colourful and eye-catching cover page. It beautifully captures the essence of the book and just looking at it makes me happy.

Printed in Great Britain
by Amazon